MORE PRAISE FOR *Staying Clean & Sober*

"Thank you, Millers, for putting in one convenient book everything
we tell the clients at Sacramento County Drug Court, and more!
You've created not only a sourcebook for people tired of
"white-knuckling" their way through recovery, but also for
those of us providing treatment who know that brain repair is
the essential first step to release anyone from any addiction."
– *Carolyn Reuben, L.Ac., author of* Cleansing the Body, Mind, and
Spirit, *and President, Community Addiction Recovery Association*

"A courageous step forward from two pioneers in the substance abuse
field who have worked long and hard to present this new technology
with a great voice. This important work in the integration of alternative
treatment modalities for chemical dependency is long overdue."
– *Stan Stokes, Executive Director of Bridging the Gaps*

"The Millers are exceptional communicators and educators in the
addiction field. This book offers groundbreaking, life-saving
information for anyone involved in recovery."
– *Dr. James Braly, author of* Dr. Braly's Food Allergy
and Nutrition Revolution

"Addiction treatment works, but comprehensive (complementary)
treatment works better! This book is a marvelous way to
keep what you've got or to get what you need."
– *Dr. Jay M. Holder, President, American College of Addictionology &
Compulsive Disorders*

"Merlene and David are far ahead of their time. They are among the
first to finally change the way we treat addiction in this country."
– *Tamea Sisco, D.D., C Ad*

Other Books by Merlene Miller and David Miller

STAYING SOBER: A GUIDE FOR RELAPSE PREVENTION
by Terence T. Gorski and Merlene Miller

LEARNING TO LIVE AGAIN: A GUIDE FOR RECOVERY FROM CHEMICAL
DEPENDENCY
by Merlene Miller, Terence Gorski, and David Miller

OVERLOAD: ATTENTION DEFICIT DISORDER AND
THE ADDICTIVE BRAIN
by David Miller and Kenneth Blum

REVERSING THE WEIGHT GAIN SPIRAL
by Merlene Miller and David Miller

COUNSELING FOR RELAPSE PREVENTION
by Terence Gorski and Merlene Miller

REVERSING THE REGRESSION SPIRAL
by Merlene Miller and David Miller

Staying Clean & Sober

Complementary and Natural Strategies for Healing the Addicted Brain

Merlene Miller, M.A., & David Miller, Ph.D.

WOODLAND
PUBLISHING

Library of Congress Cataloging-in-Publication Data
Miller, Merlene.
   Staying clean & sober : complementary and natural strategies for healing
the addicted brain / Merlene Miller & David Miller.-- 1st ed.
      p. cm.
   Includes bibliographical references and index.
   ISBN 1-58054-391-X (alk. paper)
1. Substance abuse--Alternative treatment. 2. Drug addicts--Rehabilitation.
3. Alcoholics--Rehabilitation. I. Title: Staying clean and sober. II. Miller,
David K. III. Title.
   RC564.M538 2005
   616.86'06--dc22
                                                      2005011273

For ordering information or correspondence, contact:
Woodland Publishing, 448 East 800 North, Orem, Utah 84097
Please visit our website:
www.woodlandpublishing.com

Note: The information in this book is for educational purposes only and is
not recommended as a means of diagnosing or treating an illness. All matters
concerning physical and mental health should be supervised by a health practitioner knowledgeable in treating that particular condition. Neither the pub-
lisher nor author directly or indirectly dispenses medical advice, nor do they
prescribe any remedies or assume any responsibility for those who choose to
treat themselves.

ISBN 1-58054-391-X
Printed in the United States of America

Contents

Acknowledgments

We HAVE HAD help in writing this book. And the message we share reflects the words and works of the dedicated people we consider part of our team. There is Jim Braly, who has caught the vision for the future of IV amino acid therapy and given so much to make it a reality; Stan Stokes at Bridging the Gaps in Winchester, Virginia, where comprehensive treatment is available; Jay Holder, who is committed not only to providing the tools of amino acid therapy, auriculotherapy, and torque release to enhance the recovery of the people he treats at Exodus Treatment Center in Miami but also to those he trains in these procedures; Julia Ross at Recovery Systems in Mill Valley, California, who felt for many years that she was a lone voice crying out for better treatment with amino acid therapy; Tamea Sisco, who took the risk to begin IV amino acid therapy at Excel Treatment Center in Denver before anyone had paved the way; Carol Cummings in Wichita, Jeff Holbrook in Idaho Falls, and Dee Ogle in Corpus Christi, who have believed there is a better way and shared our dreams all along the way. The voices of these people are in this book and their work has led the way and guided us in our search for better treatment. We also want to thank others who have shared with us information about their work and/or research: Joel Lubar, Kathy Sloan, Diana Guthrie, Richard Guthrie, Bill Hitt, Carolyn Reuben, Charley Gant, Karen Hurley, and Kenneth

Blum. A very special thanks goes to our agent Stephanie von Hirschberg, who has believed in the value of this book from the beginning and given us endless help and encouragement. We thank our editor at Woodland Publishing, Cord Udall, and those who assisted him. Thanks to those who assisted in manuscript preparation: Teah Sloan, June Wright, Jan Sloan, Paul Kennard, and Jane Heywood. We are grateful to special friends who have supported us through our journey: Anne and Al Brady, Marilyn and John Shank, Terry and Hubert Rathbun, The Harrison Group, Dick and Jane Heywood, Anne Barcus, Dr. Ben and everyone at Bridging the Gaps. Our wonderful family is always supportive and assists us in any way they can. Thanks to our parents, our sons, our daughters-in-law, and our grandchildren. And, of course, Sammy.

Foreword

by Dr. James Braly

THERE ARE HUNDREDS of thousands of grateful, sober individuals who credit treatment based on the principles of Alcoholics Anonymous for their successful recovery from addiction. For these people, conventional treatment has provided important tools for attaining abstinence and the long-term prevention of relapse. Unfortunately, 70–85 percent of those receiving conventional psychosocial counseling—and more recently prescription drug therapy—for addiction continue to relapse within the first six to twelve months (approximately 50 percent in the first thirty days, two-thirds within ninety days).

These are individuals in desperate need of innovative, science-based, safe and effective, long-term solutions. And that is precisely what best-selling authors Merlene and David Miller offer in this thoughtfully provocative, path-breaking book.

A few years ago, while living in Mexico the Millers observed with amazement the use of intravenous amino acid therapy for patients going through acute withdrawal from alcohol and a variety of other drugs. (I had used a similar therapy with great success back in the 1980s with patients suffering acute withdrawal from the abrupt elimination of allergic foods, caffeine and alcohol). Since then, the Millers and I have worked together to refine and clinically test a similar intravenous amino acid formula with equal success in sober but severely symptomatic addicts. Amino acid therapy is presented in this book along with many other promising advances. (My two favorite chapters are the ones discussing use of oral amino acid supplementation and auriculotherapy—electrical, needle-less acupuncture of the ear. These two chapters alone are worth the price of the book). A new technique, originated by Dr. Jay Holder, is also presented, called chiropractic torque release. The Millers have also seen great results with brain wave biofeedback. By combining amino acid therapy with auriculotherapy and other techniques discussed in this book the thirty day relapse-free rate is reportedly now approaching 90 percent, compared to a 30–50 percent failure rate utilizing the orthodox approach. Very exciting stuff, indeed!

The Millers are more than qualified to write this revolutionary book. I have worked closely with them and they are personal friends. They've "walked their talk," with David celebrating his thirtieth year of sobriety from alcohol last year (2004). He has also significantly and permanently lessened his chronic abstinence symptoms ("white knuckling," a syndrome extremely common among sober alcoholics) by daily supplementing with key amino acids as presented in depth in Chapter 4.

Merlene and David have their fingerprints seemingly everywhere in the addiction field. They've constantly searched for and reported ways of improving what is and implementing what needs to be. To boot, they are best-selling authors with an amazing close to one million copies of their books sold to date. The reason for their success as authors is that they are both exceptional communicators and educators, renowned for their ability to take important, but often difficult concepts, and magically present them in a crystal clear, simple-to-understand "Milleresque" style. In addition to being scholars who know their subject, they are caring people who genuinely want to share what they have learned with those who need it most—those who have experienced the pain of addiction in their own lives or in the life of a loved one.

Who should read this book?

• All counselors, therapists and health care providers unfamiliar with the advancements in alternative therapies for addictions.

• All individuals who, having achieved sobriety, remain chronically symptomatic.

• All individuals with a long history of repeated relapses.

• Those of you who have loved ones in the iron grasp of addictions.

• And those among you who would like a sneak preview of how the field of addiction will be routinely practiced a decade or two from now.

If you are interested in promising, provocative and practical ideas about becoming and staying "clean" from addiction, you will thoroughly enjoy reading and implementing the therapies and principles contained in this practical and well-constructed guide.

James Braly, M.D., has specialized in alternative and nutritional treatments for numerous chronic conditions, including addiction. He was the lead physician for a widely acclaimed naturopathic medical practice, and has served as technical advisor for several companies and organizations. Dr. Braly is also the author of several successful health titles, including Dr. Braly's Food Allergy and Nutrition Revolution.

CHAPTER 1

The Search for Better Treatment

WHEN I MET David Miller, he was an active alcoholic. I didn't recognize it because, as he has often said, I knew so little about alcoholism that I thought withdrawal was talking with a "Southern accent." I thought he drank too much, but I wasn't planning to marry him. I figured it was his business. But both those factors changed. What had been a close friendship developed into a deep love; and a life crisis caused him to make the decision to quit drinking. As far as I was concerned, the drinking problem was over and we were in love, so we got married.

His period of abstinence didn't last very long. And living with his drinking instead of observing it as an outsider was more of a problem than I knew how to deal with. I had four children from a previous marriage and ultimately felt I had to ask him to choose between us and his drinking. He chose us and began attending Alcoholics Anonymous. But his decision to stop drinking was just the beginning of our struggles. I thought that if he weren't drinking everything should be fine. I didn't realize that there are symptoms of addiction that emerge with abstinence that can make life nearly as uncomfortable as the drinking (and are now thought by many authorities to precede and contribute to addiction in the first place).

Without alcohol, David was moody, stress sensitive, and irritable. He was highly sensitive to noise (and all of my children are hearing impaired, resulting in a noisier than usual environment). And he sometimes found family life almost unbearable. He often withdrew from the rest of us, leaving me feeling depressed and rejected. Sometimes I felt it had been easier to live with him when he was drinking.

In spite of this, I respected his effort to maintain sobriety even when I could see it was very, very difficult for him. I tried to be supportive and he tried to give as much to the marriage as he was able. But sometimes the internal turmoil became so unbearable that he drank. For three years he struggled to maintain sobriety (and periodically slipped) before he was able to maintain ongoing abstinence. He now has thirty years of continuous recovery.

His years of sobriety are due somewhat to managing what we later called the abstinence-based symptoms of addiction. In all the meetings we attended, the counseling we received, and reading we did, no one told us it would be so difficult. No one told us that these symptoms are frequently a part of recovery. And no one told us what to do about them, quite frankly, *because no one really knew.*

We struggled with the effects of David's abstinence, learning by trial and error to cope with them. For instance, we noticed that the symptoms were worse on Saturdays. Why? As we examined what was different we found a number of culprits. He slept later on Saturdays, and thus ate later. In fact, he would often just get up and go to his AA sponsor's house without eating. There he would drink coffee, eat doughnuts, and smoke cigarettes. And when he came home, it was to find me vacuuming, the kids playing music, the phone ringing, and general chaos reigning. His only way of coping with the noise was to leave, which I resented. So when he did come back, even if things had settled down, I was usually not in a loving, supporting mood.

Eventually, because our desire to make our marriage better was so strong, we began to search for answers to the problems linked to David's fight with sobriety. Some of the steps we took were very simple. I began taking a glass of orange juice to him before he got out of bed in order to raise his blood sugar (and though I didn't realize it at the time, to temporarily alter his brain chemistry). He started eating breakfast before he went to see his sponsor and refrained from the doughnuts and limited the coffee. Almost immediately, he was amazed at how different he felt. When he came home he was in a better mood, and I tried to reduce the typical noise and clamor. David made more of an effort to "stick around" and contribute to the Saturday needs of the family. But if things did become too stressful, I tried to understand his need to get away for a time.

Gradually, David and I discovered other ways to help him maintain a more comfortable sobriety. We found ways to reduce noise levels in the home. We discovered that you can't just work at recovery. You have to play, too. We learned that there must be creative and enjoyable activities to replace the void left by the absence of alcohol. What we were doing, but didn't realize at the time, was finding ways to alter the chemicals in the brain that help us feel good, the chemicals related to addiction—endorphins, enkephalins, serotonin, dopamine, and GABA.

Because of our efforts, we were not only able to hold our marriage together, but we also built a stronger relationship by working together to figure out how to live in sobriety. The point of David's story is that long-term, lasting sobriety is difficult. It is not just a matter of will power and self-discipline.

It is not just a choice to stop using and go on with your life. What we came to understand was that addiction is a physiologically and biochemically linked condition and that there are physiological and biochemical symptoms that can't be ignored. We realized that when recovering addicts relapse it is usually not because they don't want to stay sober—it's because *they don't know how.*

What we learned by our own trial and error, and a lot of heartache, we wanted to share with other people in recovery. We determined to help others find alternatives to relapse and to the pain that often accompanies abstinence. To do that, we began looking for better and better ways to smooth out the road to recovery.

After a few years of ongoing recovery, David went back to school and became an addiction counselor. He was fortunate to work with Terry Gorski, who was also interested in the issue of relapse prevention. Terry was looking at what he called post-acute withdrawal, a group of symptoms he had found often accompanied abstinence. It was a relief to have a name for the symptoms David experienced and to realize that he was not alone. These were common in sobriety.

Together, Terry, David, and I wrote a book called *Learning to Live Again, A Guide to Recovery from Alcoholism* (later revised and called *Learning to Live Again, A Guide to Recovery from Chemical Dependency*). In this book we were able to share what we had learned about the road to recovery and how to make it smoother. More importantly, we were excited to realize that other people could benefit from what we had learned the hard way.

Later, Terry and I wrote a book called *Staying Sober, A Guide to Relapse Prevention.* This book has been used widely in the addiction field since 1986. The reason for its wide acceptance is that for the first time people who read the book began learning about symptoms that make recovery difficult.

They realized that they are not crazy or hopeless if they have these symptoms or if they relapse.

In *Staying Sober* we say that post-acute withdrawal symptoms are due to damage to the nervous system from drug use and will go away as the brain and body heal. But what began to trouble David after a time was that for many people the symptoms never go away. In fact, they had never gone away for him—he had just learned how to cope with them. After more than ten years of sobriety, these effects could still make him very uncomfortable.

Soon enough, David and I had developed our own treatment program, and clients told us they still suffered the symptoms after many years of sobriety. Because we specialized in relapse prevention, most of the individuals we worked with struggled with the symptoms and with periodic relapse. We realized that for some people recovery is not a road but a mountain. Consequently, we developed our own strategy of relapse prevention and applied it to a variety of conditions, including food addiction. Eventually, we wrote a book, *Reversing the Weight Gain Spiral*, about preventing relapse by compulsive overeaters.

As we educated clients about post-acute withdrawal symptoms, many of them informed us that they had been experiencing these symptoms *before* they started drinking or using drugs (or overeating). They had had them as long as they could remember. And they told us that these symptoms were the reason they started drinking or using drugs in the first place, as a sort of self-medication for their discomforts.

All in all, David became convinced that what we were calling post-acute withdrawal, in many cases, was not really withdrawal, but rather the return of *pre-existing* symptoms that had been relieved by addictive use. He was especially sure of this in relation to the symptoms of heightened sensitivity to noise and lights and even touch. He began to learn more about this symptom, often called "stimulus augmentation" (or sometimes "hyper-augmentation" or "hypersensitivity"). He was further interested in this condition because he had been plagued with it since he was a child.

David found that most chronic relapsers had stimulus augmentation. He discovered that people with attention deficit hyperactivity disorder (ADHD) frequently have this symptom and that sufferers of ADHD often have alcohol and drug problems. He was ultimately diagnosed with attention deficit disorder himself, and later, with scientist Kenneth Blum, wrote the book *Overload, Attention Deficit Disorder and the Addictive Brain.*

Through more research, David also discovered that many people in recovery from addiction have undiagnosed attention deficit disorder. Eventually, he learned that there are other related disorders that predispose one to addiction, among them Tourette syndrome, obsessive compulsive disorder, depression, and conduct disorder. All these conditions are neurological and biochemical. They originate from and are related to chemical imbalances in the brain. The more David and I analyzed the research related to addiction, the more aware we became of the gap between what is known about addiction and what is being done about it. As scientific research has taught us more and more about the nature of addiction, treatment has not changed—or has changed very little—to utilize new information.

If addiction is related to brain chemistry, then it seemed to us that to effectively treat addiction we had to find more effective and natural ways to alter the brain's chemistry. David and I began investigating alternative therapies that could be used to restore healthy brain chemistry, thereby aiding addicts in their recovery: nutrition, auricular therapy, acupuncture, and brainwave biofeedback (neurofeedback) are but a few.

David decided to begin by taking amino acid tablets: phenylalanine, tyrosine, and glutamine, formulated with certain vitamins. The results were amazing—he experienced significant relief from his symptoms. This made perfect sense because brain chemicals are produced, in large part, from amino acids and vitamins, and addiction and attention deficit hyperactivity disorder are, of course, related to brain chemistry.

Because of the remarkable changes resulting from the amino acid formulation, David began recommending them to addiction clients, most of whom also experienced positive results. The right combination of amino acids and vitamins delivered to the brain of the addict can restore the neurotransmitter balance, bringing a sense of well-being and relief from craving.

Eventually, we heard about a clinic in Mexico that was claiming great success over a fifteen-year period using intravenous amino acid therapy to treat addiction. We checked this out and ended up spending many months there observing addicts as they successfully withdrew from a variety of different drugs.

There are now numerous clinics in the United States that offer intravenous amino acids for the treatment of addiction. In our opinion, this is the most effective and remarkable treatment we have encountered. David and I have observed patients going through detoxification from heroin, alcohol, and cocaine use with relatively little discomfort. We have seen them emerge from their mental fog alert and feeling good within days. One of the most remarkable things about amino acid therapy is that many patients report that all craving for the addictive substance disappears. In addition, many indicate that they feel better than they have ever felt, suggesting that they had suffered from amino acid and vitamin deficiencies most of their lives.

Through our association with the clinic in Mexico, Kenneth Blum, Charles Gant, Julia Ross, Tamea Sisco, Jay Holder, and the program at Bridging the Gaps we have observed or reviewed hundreds of cases in which people have benefited from the use of amino acid therapy and believe strongly that it is the best kept secret in the treatment of addiction and hope to help spread the word so that many more can benefit.

While searching for more effective treatments, we found that other neurological treatments for the brain are currently being used successfully to help addicts overcome the craving for alcohol or drugs. Hundreds of drug courts throughout the United States have found that auriculotherapy or ear acupuncture is more effective than traditional methods alone. Brainwave biofeedback has been found to be successful in changing brainwave patterns. This allows the individuals to choose to increase brainwaves that help them relax or concentrate better. Many people find therapeutic massage to be relaxing, soothing, and good for the body.

Sometime along our journey to find better treatment for the physical symptoms of addiction, we began to lose sight of the importance of the psychological and spiritual needs of the recovering person. The clinic in Mexico had no counseling program, and the emphasis was strictly on changing the brain chemistry with IV amino acids alone. The clinics' patients felt so good from the treatment that they believed they were cured forever. Consequently, even though they were advised to get follow-up treatment, most did not. Almost always when patients returned for more amino acid treatment because they had relapsed, they had not sought follow-up treatment that would have helped them with the other aspects of recovery. We found the same thing true of many of the programs that utilized brainwave biofeedback, nutrition, or acupuncture. We realized that treating the brain alone without addressing emotional and spiritual needs is in some ways as incomplete as treatment that does not provide healing for the brain.

We have seen, in recent years, as more scientific information has become available about the biochemical nature of addiction, a growing tendency to treat it with prescription medications. While medications do address the physiology of addiction, we see this as a step in the wrong direction because

- in most cases, they do not treat the underlying problem;
- they often have side effects that become problems themselves or cause the person to stop taking them;
- they can become a new addiction;
- and perhaps most important, they can pose a danger if people relapse with the medication in their system creating a synergistic effect in the body that can be very harmful, even deadly.

For these reasons we do not present prescription medication as one of the strategies we recommend for healing the addicted brain. It should only be used as a last resort, and then with a great deal of caution.

This book is the culmination of what we have learned so far regarding complete and lasting addiction recovery. We have searched for explanations as to why addiction recovery is so difficult, as well as treatments that could effect changes that could make it less so. The following points summarize what we have come to believe as a result of our journey:

- Addiction is primarily a disease of the brain, and the biochemical imbalances associated with it create chronic, abstinence-based symptoms that often lead to relapse.
- For many people, staying sober and free from drugs means living with emotional pain—anxiety, confusion, and depression (in fact, 25 percent of recovering alcoholics are reported to eventually commit suicide)—unless proper brain chemistry is restored.
- Treatment that addresses only the psychological, social, and spiritual issues connected with addiction is effective less than 20 percent of the time. Complete treatment for addiction

requires marrying biochemical treatment for the brain with counseling and education to support lifestyle change.

- Alternative therapies for healing the brain are being used with great success—in particular, intravenous and oral delivery of amino acids, with a recovery rate of 70–75 percent—but unfortunately, few people know about them.
- Healing of the brain must be supported by emotional and spiritual healing.
- Self-care and relapse prevention are essential for ongoing comfortable sobriety.

We are witnessing the birth of what we have long searched for. We are now entering a new era of treatment. The work being done now is pioneer work and, for us, the search for more effective treatment goes on. Amino acid therapy, brain-wave biofeedback, and auricular therapy, along with nutritional therapy, counseling, and good life management skills, are enabling many recovering addicts to not only avoid relapse but enjoy a comfortable and healthy sobriety as well.

Perhaps you suffer from alcoholism or drug addiction for which you have found no effective treatment. Perhaps you are a parent, spouse, child or friend of an addict, and are living a life of quiet desperation, believing your loved one is hopelessly addicted and can never return to healthful living. Or perhaps you are an addiction professional who, while doing all you know to give life back to people who are addicted, is contiunally facing the reality that most of your clients are relapsing because the treatment you offer has not provided relief from the discomfort that often accompanies abstinence. We hope the message of this book will open the door to new options and new hope for you.

CHAPTER 2

This Is Your Brain on Drugs; This Is Your Life on Drugs

NO ONE INTENDS to become addicted. No child says, "I'm going to be an alcoholic when I grow up." No adolescent who experiments with drugs thinks, "I want to become a junkie." No one, when taking the first puff, drink, sniff, or injection, plans on getting addicted to cigarettes, alcohol, marijuana, glue, speed, cocaine, prescription medication, or heroin.

Yet for a great number of people, that first drink or hit deceptively leads to physical dependence. It is impossible for anyone who has never been addicted to comprehend the power of addiction. It seems logical and reasonable to stop doing something so harmful to yourself and others, especially those you care about most.

But addicts do not "think" about their drug use from the part of their brain that is reasonable and logical. Instead, the addiction is fueled by the component of their brain that is concerned with survival—the limbic system—the same component that tells us to eat, drink, flee or fight. In essence, the limbic system is the part of the brain that is concerned with keeping us alive. It monitors the body's need for survival, and when it senses our survival is dependent on a certain behavior, it creates a compulsion so strong that it becomes extremely difficult to resist taking that action. Without it we might forget to breathe or eat or reproduce.

This part of the brain tells addicts that they must have the addictive substance or they will die (and in some cases, that really is true). This part of the brain controls the thinking of the addicted person even after the pleasure of drinking or taking drugs has been replaced by severe pain.

Patty, a cocaine addict struggling unsuccessfully to overcome her addiction, describes it this way: "It seems like I have two brains. There is the brain that tells me that if I use cocaine, I am going to be miserable; it's not fun anymore; it's not worth it; afterward, I'll feel guilt and remorse and be deeper in debt. The other brain says that I really need this; I have to have it; something worse than death will happen to me if I don't have it; I deserve it; and this time I might get back the old feeling that I need so badly. This argument goes on until the brain in favor of using cocaine convinces the other one that I probably will end up doing it anyway so I may as well go ahead and do it early so I won't be up all night and unable to work the next day. For some reason this makes sense to my other brain and I go get some coke."

But how does a person get to this point at which the survival part of the brain overrules the reasoning part? And why does it happen to some people who drink alcohol, smoke marijuana, or try cocaine and not happen to others who do the same thing?

Let us tell you a little about James and Richard. They are

brothers, and David and I have known them since they were young. As teenagers they used drugs together. In fact, they used the same drugs in the same quantities. But as they reached college age James realized that his drug use was interfering with what he wanted out of life. He quit using illegal drugs, though he continued to drink infrequently and always in moderation.

By the same age Richard realized that what he wanted out of life *was* drugs. James enrolled in college, established a career, had a family, and became a politically active and respected member of his community. Richard also enrolled in college, many times, in fact; but he never completed a semester before some drug-related incident interfered and caused him to drop out. He married a couple of times, but when his wives eventually asked him to choose between them and drugs, he chose drugs. He is now in prison, serving an eighteen-month sentence for possession of cocaine.

What was different in these brothers? Why the different paths taken, despite the similarities in their drug abuse? To answer this we need to examine what normally happens in the brain and what differs in some people that predisposes them to using and becoming addicted to mood-altering substances.

The Reward System of the Brain[1]

We all seek physical and emotional comfort. We want to feel good. It is well established that the action of chemicals in the brain (neurotransmitters) play a significant role in feelings of pleasure and well-being. Manufactured and stored within brain cells (neurons), neurotransmitters act as messengers to carry messages from one neuron to another. When a neuron receives a stimulus (by something we see, hear, feel, smell, think, imagine or perceive), it sends a chemical message across the synapse (the space between neurons) to receptor sites on the next neuron, which sends the message on to the next. Each neuron, reaching out like the branches of a tree, connects with thousands of others, all of which are sending and receiving neurochemical messages from one to another.

Neurotransmitters are chemical messengers that mediate mood, emotion, thought, behavior, motivation, and memories. When neurotransmitters are present in optimal amounts, we have feelings of well being. Neurotransmitters work together in harmony to create feelings of pleasure to reward us for certain behaviors that help keep us alive and comfortable. A deficiency or excess of any neurotransmitter will give rise to uncomfortable feelings.

Neurotransmitters are manufactured in the brain's neurons from amino acids. (Remember that, because we will soon be talking about the importance of amino acids in healing the addicted brain.) Serotonin, dopamine, norepinephrine, gamma-aminobutyric acid (GABA), taurine, and the opioid peptides (endorphins, enkephalins, and dynorphins, often collectively called opioids), and glutathione are key neurotransmitters significantly involved in the addiction process.

Serotonin

Serotonin improves one's ability to concentrate and boosts feelings of well-being, relaxation, satiation, and security. Low levels can result in depression, sleep problems, poor concentration, confusion, aggressiveness and violence, sugar or carbohydrate cravings, and increased sensitivity to pain. (See the serotonin deficiency questionnaire in Appendix B.)

Dopamine

Dopamine and its derivative norepinephrine increase alertness, heightened awareness, wakefulness, and a sense of vitality and energy. They speed up the thought process and improve muscle coordination. Low levels give rise to lethargy and weakness, depression, tremors and other movement disorders associated with Parkinson's disease, and many of the symptoms of attention deficit hyperactivity disorder. High levels can result in anxiety, fear, excessive energy, violence, and even schizophrenia and paranoia. When serotonin is low and dopamine is high, you can feel depression and anxiety at the same time.

Opioids

The opioid peptides—endorphins, enkephalins, and dynorphins—are powerful natural pain relievers. They are overproduced in response to pain and physical exertion and block the transmission of pain signals at the receptor site. They also combine with other neurotransmitters to produce feelings of euphoria.

GABA

Popularly referred to as the body's natural tranquilizer, GABA helps to relax the mind, reduce anxiety, and keep stress-related nerve impulses at bay. Normally, the brain produces all the GABA we need, but environmental factors can result in depleted levels of GABA. Too little of this important compound can result in anxiety, irritability, and insomnia. While GABA is sometimes called "the natural valium of the brain," author and clinician Dr. Charles Gant has said that it should be stated the other way around—that valium should be called the unnatural GABA, because valium can only temporarily make you feel the way you would if your brain were producing adequate amounts of GABA.

Once released, neurotransmitters seek out and attach to adjacent neurons that have receptors with a complementary shape. The neurotransmitters fit into the receptors in the same way a key fits into a lock; and receptors will accept only those neurotransmitters with a corresponding shape. To really understand the addiction process, it is important to understand that the receptors will also accept ingested mood-altering chemicals that mimic natural brain chemicals.

The interactions of neurotransmitters have a powerful effect on our emotions and thinking. Some of these natural neurochemicals act as stimulators, some as inhibitors. As these stimulators and inhibitors act upon one another, the chemical cascade that forms is intended to result in a feeling of pleasure. Most of the actions we take are chosen because they produce this feeling of reward. We eat because it produces a reward of satiation and pleasure. We eat *certain* foods because they produce a better reward than others (chocolate produces more reward for most people than does parsley). We have sex because it creates a powerful release of pleasure-producing chemicals. We work because the work itself is rewarding for us or because the end result produces a reward. We refrain from certain actions because they do not produce the feeling of reward we are seeking.

When the reward system of the brain is working properly it creates a sense of well-being, pleasure and satisfaction with normal activities. When our needs are met, our brain rewards us. Simple as that. A word of praise for a job well-done acts as a stimulus that activates a chemical reaction in the brain that feels good. A hug from a loved one sets off a brain chemical interaction that acts as a reward.

The way we think, feel, and behave results from chemical interactions in the brain and, in turn, produces additional chemical reactions in the brain. When the result of an action is positive, it reinforces that behavior and motivates us to repeat it. We tend to repeat actions that cause us to feel relaxed, happy, satisfied, euphoric, and fulfilled.

What produces these rewards is different for different people. Chocolate may produce more reward for one person while potato chips may produce more reward for someone else. Reading a novel may be rewarding for someone, while waterskiing may produce more reward for another. We all differ in what gives us satisfaction and in the depth of satisfaction we experience. Ultimately, though, we are all alike in that we are motivated by chemical actions in the brain that nature uses to keep us motivated, functioning, reproducing and ultimately alive.

But what happens if and when this reward system does not work properly?

Reward Deficiency[2]

Some scientists use the term *reward deficiency* to describe a condition in which the reward system of the brain is not working properly, thereby resulting in a lack of reward for normal activities. The body seeks a neurochemical balance, and, when there is too much of one neurotransmitter or not enough of another, the brain sends out a powerful message to right the imbalance.

This imbalance of neurotransmitters can result in a reward deficiency that can manifest as restlessness, anxiety, "emptiness," lack of satisfaction, and vague or specific cravings. This is the brain's message to us to take action to right the imbalance. People with this deficiency may feel as if they are constantly in need of something to fill the emptiness, reduce the anxiety, elevate the mood, quiet the restlessness, or satisfy the cravings.

There are numerous causes of reward deficiency in the

brain. Many people are born with a genetic impairment that interferes with normal brain chemical balances and interactions. Numerous genes have been identified that are associated with conditions that manifest as symptoms of reward deficiency. Among the genetic conditions associated with reward deficiency are attention deficit hyperactivity disorder (ADHD), Tourette syndrome, and obsessive compulsive disorder. And this is a key point: many people born with genetic reward deficiency are also genetically predisposed to becoming addicted.

Jan's father was an alcoholic. Although she was not aware of it at the time, she realizes now that he also had attention deficit hyperactivity disorder (ADHD). (Later, she was diagnosed with ADHD as an adult recovering alcoholic.) In remembering her childhood, she recalls that she was always restless and anxious, had difficulty concentrating, was easily stressed, and was distracted by noise and competing sounds. She remembers that she never felt comfortable, at ease, or satisfied. She believed there was something seriously wrong with her, but she had no idea what it was. She just knew from an early age that she was different. It wasn't until she discovered alcohol in her early teens that she began to fit in and feel comfortable and satisfied.

Although the risk of addiction is very high among those genetically predisposed, reward deficiency from non-genetic causes can put a person at high risk for addiction. The normal process of neurotransmission can be altered by environmental conditions as well as genetic.

Prenatal conditions such as alcohol or drug use by the mother, malnutrition, or injury during pregnancy can result in a lifetime of impaired brain chemistry.

Malnutrition over an extended time (caused by very low calorie dieting, the unavailability of food, food allergy/food insensitivity, or a diet lacking in adequate nutrition) can impair the proper production and interaction of brain chemicals. Neurotransmitters are, after all, produced from amino acids, vitamins and minerals, most of which are derived from food. When these precursor or "building block" nutrients are lacking, the neurotransmitter system breaks down.

Severe or ongoing stress can do long-term damage to the reward system of the brain. This may be in the form of a single traumatic event (being in an earthquake or witnessing a murder), intermittent or chronic stressful events (child abuse), a series of highly stressful situations (a death followed by a serious injury followed by loss of a job), or an ongoing condition of unrelenting stress (living with an alcoholic or drug addicted person). The importance of extreme stress in relation to altered brain chemistry cannot be overstated. The biochemical reaction to stress is normal and protective. With normal stress, these biochemicals return to normal as the stress passes. But when stress is severe or prolonged, these chemical levels may never return to normal. And a condition of chronic stress sets the stage for the use of mood-altering substances to relieve or escape from stress. An example of this may be the high number of female addicts who also were sexually abused before becoming addicts.

Physical trauma, particularly to the head, can also lead to an imbalance in neurochemicals. Richard, the brother described earlier in this chapter, suffered head trauma at age six, and it was after that that he began showing some of the characteristics that distinguished him from his brother James.

Significant heavy or long-term use of mood-altering substances can alter brain chemistry. So people who may not have the gene or be malnourished or traumatized may develop reward

deficiency just by their continued use of mood-altering substances. If James had used drugs long enough and heavy
enough he may have altered his brain chemistry as well. This
is important to the question of who becomes addicted and
who doesn't.

As we discussed earlier, for the most part, people who
become addicted have some level of genetic predisposition for
it. But that doesn't mean that someone who does not have the
genetic predisposition cannot become addicted. It depends
upon the addictive nature of the substance, the frequency and
quantity of use, and the susceptibility of the person.

There are some substances that are addictive to almost anyone who uses them. Nicotine is a good example. The majority
of people who smoke tobacco for any length of time become
addicted and find it very difficult to quit. Nicotine is considered by many researchers to be more addictive than crack
cocaine (unlike alcohol, which is only addictive to about one
out of ten people who drink). However, there are some people
who smoke without becoming addicted. They do not smoke
heavily and when they decide to quit, they throw away their
cigarettes and never pick them up again. These people cannot
understand why other people cannot do the same. There are
others, usually individuals with a certain genetic makeup for
whom smoking is extremely addictive. These people start
smoking at a younger age and find it so difficult to quit that
repeated efforts prove futile. They need to be aware that they
are not weak willed. In fact, it has been demonstrated that
many smokers who quit temporarily and relapse experience
major depression, depression they experienced before their
first smoke. Smoking is a way of self-medicating the depression. The cessation of smoking unmasks the underlying
depressive state. Simply put, these people need extra help, and
some of the measures in this book should be helpful for them.

Whether the cause of reward deficiency is genetic or environmental, it puts individuals at higher risk for beginning to use a substance to relieve the discomfort of the deficiency and also for becoming addicted to that substance. Let's now examine what happens when those with reward deficiency, for whatever reason, discover a substance that provides what they are missing.

Self-Medicating Reward Deficiency

When the normal process of neurotransmission is disrupted, the resulting state of discomfort can lead to use of mood-altering substances to relieve the discomfort. Remember that mood-altering substances fit the same receptor sites as the natural neurotransmitters of the brain. So if there is a deficiency of a natural brain chemical, the newly found "substance" (whether it be a drug, food, or behavior) becomes a substitute for the natural chemical, thus, at least temporarily, correcting the deficiency. Suddenly the anxiety, restlessness, "emptiness," and cravings are gone. The reward deficient person may feel relieved, *normal* for the first time in his or her life. But the substance usually does more than allow this person to feel normal. The brain is flooded with the substance, which often produces feelings of intense pleasure and euphoria.[3]

David: In a book I coauthored, *Overload: Attention Deficit Disorder and the Addictive Brain,* I describe my first experience with alcohol when I was about twelve during my uncomfortable life with reward deficiency:

While I was drinking about the third beer, my brain got very excited. It sent me the message that this was the stuff I had been searching for all my life.

Brain to rest of Dave: "Did you feel what I just felt, old buddy?"

"Yeah, what in the hell was that?"

"That, my dear boy, was the nectar of the Gods running through us like a healing stream and taking all our tensions away."

"Yeah, brain, that's what it feels like all right. Kind of like I've been washed clean of all that ails me."

That sense of relief those beers brought was a revelation. I felt free for the first time in my life. In control. I knew this was now. I was in this instant, loving this instant of time, never wanting it to go away. The present had always been my enemy, now it was my friend. Alcohol was my ticket to space travel. It was my friend, my lover . . .

Continued Use and Tolerance

Are individuals who are reward deficient more likely than the average person to continue using a mood-altering substance once they have found one that "works" for them? Of course they are. It is highly unlikely that, having discovered a way to instantly feel better, they will not do it over and over again. That is the reward they have been missing. And just as a hungry person seeks the reward of food, reward deficient people seek what will satisfy their hunger. And the reward is immediate. They don't have to wait for a payoff. It works, it works now, and it works every time (at least in the beginning). It relieves their discomfort and gives them pleasure. They are no longer reward deficient.

There are two reasons why people with reward deficiency are likely to become addicted. First is the continued and regular use of the mind-altering substance. The other is that people with genetic reward deficiency are more susceptible to becoming addicted because it seems the same genes that cause reward deficiency also cause something different to occur in their bodies when they use mood-altering substances. They metabolize the substance differently, thereby changing what happens in the brain. The experience for them is not just pleasant but exhilarating. In other words, they get a higher high.

For alcoholics, this extreme high is probably due to the interaction of high levels of acetaldehyde.[4] Individuals with a genetic predisposition to become alcoholic do not metabolize alcohol in the same way as other people. They break down the alcohol more slowly, and acetaldehyde, a normal byproduct of the breakdown of alcohol in the body, builds up to a higher level in alcoholics than in non-alcoholics. This substance makes its way to the brain and combines with different brain chemicals to produce TIQ[5] (see sidebar), a morphine-like substance that is extremely addictive. It not only enables people to feel euphoric but also enables them to function better than normal.

It is very difficult to detect addiction in the early stages because, for the people most susceptible, it seems more beneficial than harmful. It provides what their brains lack normally. Just as Ritalin (a mood-altering, amphetamine-like substance) can allow some children with attention deficit hyperactivity disorder (a reward deficiency condition) to function better, other drugs are beneficial for other reward-deficiency conditions. These drugs may make it possible to be more sociable, more at ease, and demonstrate a higher level of social skills. Physical performance may even improve. In spite of a common belief that as the quantity of alcohol consumed increases, the ability to function decreases, some people may actually be able to perform some tasks better when somewhat intoxicated than they can totally sober.

Consequently, the earliest warning sign of addiction onset (the ability to function well) interferes with early diagnosis and makes it difficult for the developing addict or others to recognize there is a problem. The ability to "handle their liquor" (or nicotine or marijuana or prescription drug) actually conceals

The Story of Tetrahydroisoquinoline (TIQ)

During World War II, because of the shortage of morphine for pain on the battlefield, a synthetic morphine was developed called tetrahydroisoquinoline (TIQ). It worked well as a painkiller, but it couldn't be used because it was too addictive. Later this same substance was found, during autopsies, in the brains of people who had died from alcoholism. It was thought to be morphine. Why would morphine be in the brains of alcoholics? This is not a natural substance produced by the body. But it was not morphine. It was TIQ. Now we know that this substance is created by a metabolic abnormality in alcoholics and people with the genetic predisposition to become alcoholic. It is created when acetaldehyde (created in excess in alcoholics when they drink) combines with brain chemicals to produce this morphine clone. Most people do not produce TIQ when they drink because with the normal metabolic process alcohol breaks down into acetaldehyde and then breaks down further in its journey out of the body. But with the alcoholic metabolic pathway the breakdown occurs more slowly and allows a build up of acetaldehyde, which finds its way to the brain, combines with natural chemicals and becomes the morphine-like substance TIQ which produces a "high" much greater than normal. For almost anyone, drinking is a pleasant experience. (That is why people drink socially.) But for people with a predisposition to become addicted, the experience is exhilarating and energizing. Once TIQ is deposited in the tissue of the brain, it does not leave. This is why alcoholics cannot learn to drink in moderation. They will never have a "normal" reaction to the ingestion of alcohol. Their brains are forever changed.

the problem and creates the belief among early stage addicts that they are immune to the painful consequences that they see others experience because of drinking or drug use. This is a disease that appears in the early stage as a benefit, allowing the person to experience the euphoria without paying any of the penalties.

All the while, the brain is changing and adapting to the regular ingestion of the drug. Early on these changes may seem beneficial. People who are becoming addicted can usually tolerate larger and larger quantities without becoming intoxicated and without experiencing harmful consequences. This is tolerance.

But over time, continued heavy use, especially by someone with a genetic predisposition, leads to addiction. As they can consume larger quantities and their bodies adapt to the presence of these large quantities, eventually they not only can but must use larger and larger quantities to get the same effect, creating more and more changes in the brain.

Jan knew from the first drink that she would continue to use alcohol to feel good. She knew immediately that it took away all the things about her that always made her feel different. At first she could drink with no problems. She could drink larger quantities than her friends could without getting drunk. She was able to function better when she had a few drinks than she could sober. She felt more free to express herself. She started writing poetry and thought she had found or released the creative side of her. She found that as she drank more, she was able to drink even more. She began to find that the amounts she had used before no longer did for her what they used to, and she increased the frequency and quantity of her drinking. She was unaware that biochemical and physical changes were taking place in her brain which were setting her up for problems. She thought she was in no danger of becoming addicted because she could "hold her liquor" better than anyone she knew. She was not aware that this was an early warning sign of alcoholism. Alcohol was her best friend and, she thought, her friend for life.

Using Addictive Substances to Relieve Their Own Painful Consequences

When substance use is heavy and continuous, the good feelings produced at first are eventually negated by the painful consequences. These consequences can come in many forms. Problems may arise from drinking and driving or other encounters with the law. There may be problems within the family or on the job. Or there may be physical complications. Whatever the problems are, the user now knows how to make the pain of them go away. Using the mood-altering substance temporarily takes away pain. But the pain soon returns and as a result, the addict, now feeling some painful consequences, uses more and more. The more pain, the more use. The need to use the substance to relieve the pain of using the substance blocks the awareness of what is really causing the pain.

What is happening in the brain, at this point, is that the mood-altering substance is interfering with the release of neurotransmitters and blocking the receptors. So with heavier use there are fewer neurotransmitters being produced and released than before. And it takes more and more of the substance to fill the receptors and get high.

Let's get back to Jan. To her surprise, she began to have problems because of her drinking. At first she did not realize that these problems had anything to do with drinking. She began skipping school and thought she was just having a good time. When she was caught and punished at home and suspended from school, she told herself everyone was just overreacting to her free spirit. She felt misunderstood and angry. What did she do? She comforted herself by drinking more.

Dependence

Addicts are unaware that physiological and biochemical changes are occurring as long as they are able to drink or get their drug. They think they are functioning normally. And they may believe they are drinking or using responsibly or at least attempting to do so. When enough problems occur, they may attempt to control their use. But by the time they are aware that their alcohol or other drug use is the problem, they cannot choose to use responsibly. As the brain adapts to higher levels of the substance, the body accepts this as normal and demands that this "normal" be maintained.

While tolerance is increasing, so is dependence. Want is transformed into need. Craving for the substance leads to continued substance use in spite of the painful consequences. The person cannot function without the substance. The person no longer uses the substance to simply feel good or to relieve the painful consequences caused by the substance. As neurons in the brain adapt to larger and larger quantities, the brain becomes reliant upon the mood-altering substance and shuts down its own production of neurotransmitters. The brain does not need to keep producing them because the receptors are being filled by ingested substances.

When the brain does not get its supply from an outside source, it does not snap into production and start supplying the needed chemicals. It screams out for more of the ingested substance. In short, it produces a feeling of intense craving. The addict now uses alcohol or other drugs only to relieve the painful consequences of not using them. This is when the survival portion of the brain takes over. It believes it must have the substance to survive. As a result, it overpowers the rational part of the brain, and obtaining the substance becomes as strong and vital a need as breathing. TV celebrity Bill Moyer has called this scenario the "hijacked brain." The drug has essentially stolen the ability of the addict to think rationally and to choose responsibly.

When Jan got married, her husband objected to her heavy drinking, so she decided she would cut back. But her attempts were short-lived. She would cut back for a few days and then soon find that she was back to her regular amount. As this became more and more of a problem in her marriage, Jan tried many ways to drink in moderation. She would set rules; however, she would eventually break them. She would promise herself she would only drink during certain times of the day. Or she would only drink only on weekends. Or she would only drink beer. Or she would drink only with other people. But it was all for naught—she broke every promise she made to her husband and herself.

Fearing her husband was going to leave her, Jan promised to quit entirely. And she did. For two days. She was sick and miserable for those two days. She never stopped thinking about drinking. She was obsessed with the idea of having "just one." The compulsion to take that one drink was overpowering. Finally, convinced she could have one and stop, she gave in and soon her drinking was out of control again. Not surprisingly, her husband did leave her, which provided her with a real reason to drink, and alcohol completely took over her life.

The Pleasure is Gone

What was once the great friend has now become an enemy. The drug no longer produces any pleasure. It creates pain, suffering and misery. Instead of being able to use more and more, addicts at this point can use less and less before becoming sick, out of control, afraid, and miserable. There is pain when using drugs and pain when not using them. The drug has depleted the brain's supply of natural feel-good chemicals and the drug is no longer a satisfactory substitute. Addicts continue to use alcohol or other drugs, not for any pleasure, but only because the survival part of the brain has taken over and believes it must have the substance or die. Attempts to stop are usually short lived and futile. Severe anxiety results when an unexpected situation interferes with the substance use or the source of supply.

At this point, many of the addict's family, friends and associates may believe he or she is behaving irresponsibly. In reality, the addict's behavior is being dictated by the survival part of the brain. It takes less and less of the substance before the person loses control and experiences symptoms of intoxication. The person may go immediately from the pain of needing the drug to the pain of using the drug. The magic is gone. The pleasure is gone. There is nothing but pain. Pain while not using the substance. Pain while using it.

Jan doesn't remember when the pleasure stopped and drinking brought her only pain. At first she thought she was so miserable because her husband had left her. Gradually she became aware that drinking was giving her no comfort. She was getting drunk more and more often. She could drink less and less before getting sick. Where had the magic gone? She was convinced she could find it again if she just looked hard enough. She tried to work at several jobs but was too sick most of the time to go to work. She was lonely and started going out with friends with whom she previously drank, those people who used to talk about her ability to hold her liquor. But now she was passing out and they were driving her home. They didn't like being with her anymore. Every day she would promise herself that tomorrow she would stop. But tomorrow she only remade the promise.

Jan eventually was able to become sober with the help of Alcoholics Anonymous. But it was the hardest thing she ever did, and now she lives one day at a time, recognizing that she can never learn to drink in moderation. Jan still grieves the loss of her best friend, alcohol. She yearns for the comfort it gave her and is looking for something else that might give her some of the pleasure she found in drinking.

Abstinence

There are times when addicted people may have a moment of sanity and realize that if they keep using, they will die. Thus, they may ask for help. They may enter a treatment center. If it is a treatment center without medical detoxification, the pain of abstinence is so severe that they frequently leave before they have made it all the way through the detoxification process. If they receive medical detoxification, many stick it out even though they are uncomfortable. But what happens now to the poor brain, totally depleted of natural brain chemicals and unable to produce an adequate supply? Usually nothing. It stays that way. Perhaps for months, perhaps for years. It is reward deficient. More extremely so than before drinking or drug use began.

What was discomfort prior to substance use now is even more intense. And the brain continues to crave the substance upon which it has come to depend. After struggling through months of pain, misery and extreme craving, many addicts give up in despair, and believing there is no way out, go back to what they know will at least relieve the craving, if not the pain.

Over a period of thirteen years Mark, a heroin addict we

met while he was getting intravenous amino acid therapy, attempted recovery many times (he thinks as many as fifty times). Sometimes he left before he got through detox and went right back to using heroin. Sometimes he made it through a 30-day treatment program and stayed clean for a while. Always during his periods of sobriety, he went to 12-step meetings. But he was totally depleted of energy. He says he was so lethargic that sometimes he couldn't get out of bed. Obviously he did not have the energy to work (he worked construction). Sometimes he thought he might have some kind of illness but nothing was ever diagnosed. Finally, believing he would never be able to function normally again, he would give up and go back to heroin. No matter how hard he tried, he was never able to maintain more than 30 days of sobriety. That is, until he received intravenous amino acid treatment, which changed his brain chemistry and offered him both relief from the pain of abstinence and energy necessary to function normally.

Now, many may say that Mark was just not motivated to get sober—that if he *really* wanted to, he could do it. But why would he go to treatment over and over again, usually voluntarily, unless he really wanted to free himself from his addiction? Remember that he had been in treatment as many as fifty times. Why would you attempt something for the fiftieth time when you had already failed forty-nine previous times if you didn't really want it? Some people might say that Mark just hadn't hurt enough yet. No, it was not the lack of pain that kept him locked into his addiction. *It was too much pain.* It was not until his brain was healed and he was relieved of his pain that he was able to live a normal life. Some people will tell you that Mark just did not have any self-discipline. How many of us have the self-discipline to endure ongoing, unrelenting pain without relief—and no relief in sight—without looking for some source of pain relief?

Let us be clear that many addicted people do make it and

find ways to maintain sobriety. Many find a better life through practicing the program of a 12-step group. Thousands of recovering addicts are living proof that sobriety and recovery from addiction are possible. Through their experience of addiction and recovery they find meaning and purpose and are able to live in serenity and peace. *We are concerned for those who do not find this path.* While some do find relief from their addictions, the majority of addicts do not. Their craving brains interfere with their ability to follow the road that has led to recovery for others.

So, for someone experiencing the discomfort and/or pleasure deficit of imbalanced neurochemistry, mood-altering chemicals do, for a period of time, work to bring relief and feelings of pleasure and well being. But eventually the good feelings of self-medication are replaced by the pain of addiction. What starts out as a rewarding experience—and perhaps an improvement in the ability to function—is transformed into a dependence on the substance in order to function. This happens as the drug further "trains" the brain to shut down production of necessary chemicals and further impairs neurological functioning. The impairment may be so severe that the person is physically, emotionally, and mentally unable to function without the drug. The need to use the drug overpowers normal reasoning and previous life values.

When the addict attempts to abstain from the substance, craving for the substance to relieve the pain of impaired neurochemistry during withdrawal leads the person back to use of the substance over and over again. Therefore, relapse is common and may lead to feelings of hopelessness and the belief that sobriety is impossible. Many addicts give up and finally experience physical, economic, and social deterioration or—too frequently—death.

Attempting recovery from addiction, then, without addressing the neurological pain and craving that accompany it, is much like attempting recovery from diabetes without addressing the functioning of the pancreas. Most treatments are helpful in that they help addicts cope with the craving and pain of abstinence, but do not take it away.

With scientific information now available, more options are becoming available to rebalance brain chemistry and restore normal neurotransmission, thus relieving the craving and discomfort of abstinence. This frees the addict to focus on other necessary tasks of recovery: rebuilding a damaged and impaired life and developing a new lifestyle that will support the maintenance of healthy brain chemistry.

Behavioral Addictions

There are two types of triggers for addiction: mood-altering substances and mood-altering activities or behaviors. The process of addiction as we have described it can result from excessive ingestion of a substance such as alcohol, cocaine, heroin, marijuana, nicotine, sugar, or any number of prescription drugs. The same process can occur as a result of excessive behaviors or activities. Behaviors that can become excessive and compulsive, and therefore addictions, include gambling or risk taking, working or achieving, excessive sexual activity, and certain eating behaviors. Behaviors involving excessive spending or compulsive saving can be included. It can be a relationship that becomes excessive or compulsive. Games— whether they be computer, video, racing, golfing or other sports—can also become addicting. It is not so much what you do as how you do it. You may wonder how an activity can bring about brain chemistry changes if nothing is ingested to bind to the receptor sites like a mood-altering substance does. The explanation lies in a better understanding of the relationship between body and mind.

All our thoughts, feelings, and actions affect brain chemistry; and brain chemistry affects our thoughts, feelings, and actions. You have no doubt heard about the "power of positive thinking." There is also power in negative thinking. Just as happy thoughts cause a release of chemicals in the body, so do angry, sad, and worrisome thoughts. Were you ever in physical or emotional pain and then smiled because of something cute your child or pet did and then realized that your pain was diminished? Were you ever feeling great and then happened to think about some disturbing situation that caused you to feel tired or perhaps develop a headache? These are examples of the power of our thoughts and feelings.

Even more powerful than thoughts and feelings are our actions. Think about a time when your child or pet did something cute and you laughed out loud. How did you feel? Research shows that a "full-body" laugh changes your brain chemistry for up to forty-five minutes. We refer to these as endogenous opioids because the release is not triggered by something you consume; it comes from within.

There are activities that change our biochemistry so much that we want to do them over and over. Some people get a biochemical response from shoplifting or inappropriate sex that is equal to or greater than a heroin injection. Nature has given us natural opioids in the brain to mediate pain. These neurotransmitters work to relieve physical as well as emotional pain. People born with the inability to feel good will look for ways to stimulate the release of these chemicals—and that often includes video games, shoplifting, gambling, inappropriate sex, and so on.

The opioids that are released from risk taking or sex are metabolized through the same dopamine pathway as cocaine or heroin or alcohol. And if the person has a reward deficit that predisposes him or her to addiction, the activity that works will be repeated as often as necessary to get the desired reward. For the person predisposed to addiction the chosen activity will rapidly proceed from self-medication to addiction.

Work addiction is fairly common in our society because overworking is applauded and rewarded. And the painful consequences of overworking may not be as apparent or recognized as activities that do not have the same kind of social payoff. But work addiction is not the same as the compulsion to *achieve*. Some people get their biochemical payoff from the act of working while other people get it from the resulting accomplishments.

Risk-taking and gambling addiction are pretty much the same addiction. That is one of the reasons that this is such a difficult behavior to control; it just changes forms. For some people gambling addiction takes the form of shoplifting or other unlawful behaviors that carry a risk of getting caught. The euphoria of shoplifting does not lie in the item taken but in the event of taking it. If the item were free, the act of taking it simply would not bring the same pleasure.

Sex addiction is what a friend of ours calls the "Bill Clinton syndrome" because Mr. Clinton is a good example of how an addiction can overcome reason. Here was a high achieving person in the throes of sex addiction risking everything of "normal" value to him in order to satisfy the need for out-of-bounds sexual activity.

Food addiction is a combination of mood-altering substances and mood-altering behaviors. Our food, of course, can contain any number of mood-altering substances; but failure to eat (anorexia) and purging (bulimia) are mood-altering activities. Karen Carpenter, the singer from The Carpenters who died as a result of anorexia and bulimia, once said that she got high from the feeling of an empty stomach. Even excessive dieting that does not reach the level of anorexia can be mood-altering and addictive.

Is It Really an Addiction?

We are often asked the question, "But aren't there positive addictions?" Well, that would depend upon your definition of addiction. According to the accepted definition and understanding of addiction, the answer to that question is "no." When we talk about addiction in this book we are talking about a condition that produces negative consequences. Continued compulsive use of a substance or engagement of an activity despite negative consequences equals addiction. You can have:

• Compulsive use with negative consequences (addiction)
• Negative consequences without compulsive use (abuse)
• Compulsive use without negative consequences (possible positive experience)

The difference between having negative consequences with and without compulsive use is the difference between a person who can easily give up the behavior and one who can't. Let's take two people who drink and drive. One goes to a party, has too much to drink, and irresponsibly gets behind the wheel and drives home. He gets stopped, arrested, and gets a ticket for driving while intoxicated. The whole experience is frightening and painful (and expensive). The next time this person goes to a party he limits how much he drinks or asks for a ride home. Another person has the same experience but instead of being a wake-up call, the incident triggers what we call denial. She blames the arresting officer, stupid laws, and difficulties at work. Under normal circumstances, we learn from our behavior, and when something is painful we tend not to repeat that behavior. But the addictive brain—which believes it must have the drug or behavior to survive—does not think rationally. It does not take the feedback it gets from reality and use that feedback to make appropriate choices. Denial is the mechanism by which reality is reshaped to conform to the need to continue using the substance or engaging in the behavior. It is only when the pain of using becomes so severe that it finally breaks through the denial that the person makes the association between actions and painful consequences. This usually occurs when those around the addict step aside and allow him to experience the full impact of an addicted life.

So, experiencing negative consequences without denial and compulsion is not addiction. It is a learning experience. But what about compulsion without negative consequences? Well, I have a compulsion to breathe. I believe I need to do that in order to survive. But that is a belief that conforms to reality. There is no denial related to it. Breathing is not an addiction. Some people have a compulsion to exercise and as long as there are no painful consequences it is not an addiction. But there are people who exercise so heavily and frequently that it causes them bodily harm and interferes with other aspects of their lives. For example, women who exercise excessively often stop menstruating, resulting in bone loss or osteoporosis. If they continue to exercise excessively despite the negative consequences, it becomes an addiction.

A Story of Addiction

Fred began drinking mouthwash when he was four or five years old. He was a restless, impulsive child. Drinking mouthwash made him feel good. When he was ten he found a bag of marijuana his father had taken from an older brother. He replaced the marijuana in the bag with parsley and smoked the marijuana. It made him feel great. From that day on he smoked marijuana daily. He knew from early childhood that mood-altering substances would be an important part of his life. But it never occurred to him that there might come a time when drugs might become an enemy rather than a friend.

Fred stayed high on marijuana or alcohol most of the time throughout his childhood. Even so, he maintained good grades with little effort. His family and teachers had no idea he was hiding such a habit. In ninth grade he began using speed (amphetamine) and crack cocaine. He was still able to function all right. He was part of a very wealthy family, so getting money for the drugs was never a problem.

Fred had only good experiences with drugs until he started using a needle. He says that nothing was ever the same again. The rush from injected drugs was the most important thing in his life. By that time he was around twenty. Soon he was speedballing (using cocaine and heroin together). Daily use caused him no problems for about nine months. Then his friend very rapidly became his enemy. There was no longer pleasure from the drugs. He was sick and miserable.

Fred knew he needed to get off the heroin and cocaine, so he decided to try treatment. He stopped using heroin and cocaine (detoxed with Librium). He continued to smoke marijuana during treatment and never intended to give up marijuana and alcohol. After eighteen days he was feeling fine and decided he didn't need any more treatment and abruptly left the treatment center. Four months later he was again injecting 3.5 grams of cocaine and 3 grams of heroin daily.

At this point Fred knew he was in deep trouble and thought there was no way out. A large inheritance made it easy to keep doing what he was doing. He came to the conclusion that he was one of those people who was on earth to "live fast and die young." He deteriorated rapidly. He was part of what he calls a "ruthless drug scene." He was sharing needles, shooting up crack. It didn't take long to go through his inheritance. So he tried working for his brother for awhile. But it was physical labor and he was in bad physical condition. He was over six feet tall, yet weighed only 155 pounds. He was weak and sweating within a half-hour of beginning work. But he had to wear long sleeves to cover the needle marks. He was always late and took bathroom breaks every twenty minutes. So much for trying to work.

By the time Fred had been injecting drugs seven years, he says he found it quite ironic that his mother was a millionaire and he had turned into a bum. "I could have had anything I wanted, but I didn't want anything but drugs." He was living in his truck, shooting up while driving. He was getting no pleasure from the drugs; he was just trying to stay alive and truly believed he would die without them. At the same time he knew he was going to die if he kept on the road he was on. Six of his friends had died within the previous year. He thought there was no way out. No hope. Just waiting to die.

Periodically Fred would see his mother to get money. One day she was crying and told him she knew what he was doing. He told her he didn't know any other way to live. She told him about a treatment she had heard about that might work for him. She begged him to try. He agreed to go "after the holidays." Four hours later he was sitting in jail. He had been stopped by the police with needles and spoons all over his truck. Though drugs were hidden in his socks, they weren't found, so he was charged with only nineteen misdemeanors. His mother posted bond and took him directly to treatment where, very near death, he received intravenous amino acid therapy.

After a few uncomfortable days Fred began to notice some remarkable changes. He had clarity of thought he had never experienced in his life. The intense cravings for the drugs seemed to have disappeared. After several months he says he can think about drugs without craving them. He feels no need for substitute drugs. Fred began attending 12-step meetings, and he has started college. He enjoys surfing and playing basketball, as well being generally physically active. Fred feels that he has a real life, which he had come to believe was impossible. He says he has goals—which he never had before. At age twenty-seven, he feels he has just been born.

CHAPTER 3

The Pain of Ineffective Treatment and Relapse

ADDICTION TO ALCOHOL and other drugs takes its toll in the lives of those who are addicted, their families, and society as a whole. It kills by overdose, by accidents, by suicides, by homicides, by destroying the mind and body, and by causing other diseases that disable and kill. It tears apart families, fills our prisons, steals our children, and drains our economy. Consider the following:[1]

- Our drug problem costs $70 billion per year, which includes legal, medical and treatment costs; cost of lost productivity on the job; the cost of drug-related crime; and the cost of social programs that address poverty, child and spouse abuse, and other social issues that result directly and indirectly from addiction.
- More than half of all persons brought into the criminal justice system suffer from some form of addiction.

- 3.5 million Americans are chronic drug users.
- One million Americans are in addiction treatment.
- There are one million drug arrests per year.
- 60 percent of all federal prisoners are drug offenders.
- 31 percent of all felony convictions in 1994 were drug offenders.
- 75 percent of all prison growth since 1980 is due to drug offenders.
- Alcohol and other drugs are associated with
    - 36 percent of child abuse
    - 52 percent of rapes
    - 62 percent of assaults
    - 20-35 percent of suicides
    - 50 percent of spousal abuse
    - 50 percent of traffic fatalities
    - 40 percent of murders
    - 88 percent of manslaughter charges
    - 69 percent of drownings
- Drug use is the overall leading cause of death in the United States.

Drug and alcohol use is listed by the government behind cancer and heart disease as a leading cause of death. But cancer death rates include lung cancer due to nicotine addiction and pancreatic and liver cancer due to alcoholism. Heart disease death rates include heart problems due to heroin and cocaine addiction. Diabetes death rates include complications because of alcoholism. Adding homicides, suicides, and accidents attributable to alcohol and drug use, it can easily be seen that alcohol and other drugs use is the leading cause of death in the nation.

Yet while progress has been made in the treatment of cancer, heart disease, and diabetes, little has been done to change the dismal rates of recovery from addiction, whether addiction to alcohol, nicotine, illegal drugs, or prescription drugs. Little or no progress has been made in the effectiveness of the treatment of alcoholism or other drug addictions in the last forty years. Although there are not consistent and accurate methods of attaining addiction recovery and relapse rates, statistics indicate that the recovery rate has not changed much in the last thirty years and claims less than a 20 percent success rate. However, there is no health problem more serious or more widespread.

Is Lack of Treatment the Problem?

Lack of available treatment is often blamed for the cost of addiction to individuals and to society. And it is true—there is a shortage of treatment. From treatment professionals, from those pushing for treatment rather than incarceration, and from those wanting more tax dollars we often hear the phrase, "Treatment works." We have even heard this from the president of the United States. But if available treatment is effective for only a small percentage of the people who get it, then we need more than additional treatment—we need better, more effective, treatment. In the treatment of addiction, it seems that we are doing the same thing over and over, trying for a different result rather than looking for better answers. You have probably heard the definition of psychotic behavior as doing the same thing over and over, expecting a different result each time. But if you always do what you always did, you'll always get what you always got.

Although there is a scarcity of treatment, this is not the major reason for the severe problems related to addiction in this country. It is the rate of *relapse* that is the major reason for the high rate of social, medical, and personal problems associated with addiction. Most people who enter conventional treatment centers will relapse, usually more than once, often repeatedly. Effective treatment would reduce relapse rates and improve the quality of sobriety, as well as reduce the myriad of problems that result from addiction.

To compound the problem, there is little understanding of this condition or how to treat it by those who most often encounter it: health professionals, human service workers, and those in the criminal justice system. Courses in addiction are seldom taught in medical schools, nursing schools, or schools of theology. Nor are they taught in psychology, social work, or criminal justice programs in colleges and universities. Addiction professionals often don't possess college degrees and draw largely from their own experience or from what has been done in the past (with a recovery rate of less than 20 percent).

While acknowledging that addiction is truly a physical disease—with profound psychological and social consequences—addiction professionals have primarily addressed the consequences, directing little treatment toward the physical disease itself or its underlying causes. They recognize that it is a disease but don't really understand how it is a disease or how it comes about and, therefore, don't know ways to treat the condition directly. *Consequently, the main goal of conventional treatment has been to teach people how to accept and cope with their symptoms.*

On the other hand, there are a few treatment centers that do focus on physical recovery, most of which, unfortunately, do not emphasize the other aspects of wellness. Addiction is a physical condition with psychological, behavioral, social, and spiritual consequences. The first step is to treat the unhealthy neurochemistry and physiology of the brain, but any treatment that ends there is incomplete. The addict is left with life deficits that cannot be overcome by fixing the brain alone. Even more of a problem is the growing tendency by health professionals to treat addiction with prescription (often mood-altering) medications. Even when used along with counseling and support groups, this practice does not improve recovery rates.

Symptoms That Interfere with the Ability to Stay Sober

Perhaps what is least understood about the nature of addiction is that there are painful symptoms that occur during abstinence that interfere with the ability to stay sober: intense and constant cravings, stress sensitivity, anxiety, dysphoria, depression, mental confusion, inability to concentrate, increased pain sensitivity, sleep disturbances, and hypersensitivity to the environment.[2]

Most people are unaware that the pain of staying sober can be, and frequently is, so severe that it interferes with the ability to function, even when the desire for and commitment to recovery is strong. This chronic discomfort is what leads to relapse.

Most addiction treatment is beneficial in the limited sense that it teaches coping skills for living with the craving and the pain of abstinence. But it does not take it away. While this approach helps many people stay sober, for the majority— those with severe abstinence symptoms—it is not enough. Some hang on, suffering all the while; some find substitute addictions; most relapse. Two out of three who enter treatment will relapse, usually within the first three to four months. Some who struggle unsuccessfully may go through treatment twenty, even fifty times. (And unfortunately, after a couple of "failures," many are refused admittance to some treatment centers.) The desire among these people to maintain sobriety is strong, so strong that they keep trying over and over again in the face of repeated "failure."

While scientific research has improved our understanding of the nature of addiction and its effect on the brain, medical and addiction professionals have applied little of this information to actually helping people get well from this devastating disease. Simply put, there is a gap between what is known about addiction and what is done about it.

The Contribution of Alcoholics Anonymous

Before Alcoholics Anonymous (AA) was started in the 1930s alcoholism was considered a hopeless condition. Rarely did anyone recover. Bill Wilson certainly seemed hopeless. He had tried all the "cures" available, but sobriety always eluded him. After becoming involved in the Oxford Group, where he became acquainted with and began to practice some principles for spiritual living, he was able to get a foothold on sobriety. But when he was sent to Akron on an extended business trip, he found himself craving alcohol and sorely tempted to take a drink. Instead he asked around to find another alcoholic and was directed to a physician, Dr. Bob, who was receptive to the message of the Oxford Group. By sharing his story, Bill was able to avoid a return to drinking, and the fellowship of Bill and Bob was the beginning of the fellowship of Alcoholics Anonymous (AA).

In the years since, AA had spread all over the world and has become the means of recovery for thousands and thousands of alcoholics. The program has been applied to other addictions in the form of Narcotics Anonymous, Overeaters Anonymous, Smokers Anonymous, Sexual Addicts Anonymous, Gamblers Anonymous and many more.

What does AA offer that has enabled so many people to become sober when they otherwise couldn't? For some it is simply the fellowship, having others available that have

The 12 Steps of Alcoholics Anonymous

1. We admitted we were powerless over alcohol, that our lives had become unmanageable.
2. Came to believe that a power greater than ourselves could restore us to sanity.
3. Made a decision to turn our will and our lives over to the care of God as we understood Him.
4. Made a searching and fearless moral inventory of ourselves.
5. Admitted to God, to ourselves, and to another human being the exact nature of our wrongs.
6. Were entirely ready to have God remove all these defects of character.
7. Humbly asked Him to remove our shortcomings.
8. Made a list of all persons we had harmed and became willing to make amends to them all.
9. Made direct amends to such people wherever possible, except when to do so would injure them or others.
10. Continued to take personal inventory and when we were wrong promptly admitted it.
11. Sought through prayer and meditation to improve our conscious contact with God, as we understood Him, praying only for knowledge of His will for us and the power to carry that out.
12. Having had a spiritual awakening as the result of these steps, we tried to carry this message to alcoholics, and to practice these principles in all our affairs.

walked the same path and are willing and available to help. For some people it is working the 12 Steps, which include acceptance of powerlessness over alcohol, willingness to accept help from a higher power, acknowledgment and confession of character defects, making amends for wrongdoings, taking regular moral inventory, promptly admitting wrongs, maintaining contact with a higher power through prayer and meditation, and carrying the message of AA to others. For many it is the combination of this change of life focus and the support of other recovering people that provides the stronghold to put one foot in front of the other until the road becomes smoother and finally joyous.[3] To contact Alcoholics Anonymous, check your local phonebook.

The Disease Model of Addiction[4]

From its earliest days Alcoholics Anonymous has embraced the concept that some people are able to drink alcohol without becoming addicted while others are not. The theory further includes the idea that those unable to control what happens when they drink must remain abstinent. This is the underlying concept that is referred to as "the disease model of addiction" and the basis of traditional treatment.

There are several hallmarks of the disease model of alcoholism. The first, as we have just stated, is that the distinction between social drinking and alcoholism lies in the person, not in the substance. Originally it was not known what it was within individuals that set them apart, but it has always been assumed that it was biological rather than psychological. It has sometimes been called an allergy, and while it is not, it is comparable to such. Most people can eat and enjoy peanuts with no problem. A few people, about one in 250, experience a dangerous reaction to peanuts (hives, difficulty breathing, severe swelling, loss of consciousness) that can even be life threatening. The difference lies in the biological make-up of people eating the peanuts.

Another basic tenet of the disease model is that once a person has become an alcoholic, that person can never learn to drink in moderation. Therefore total abstinence is necessary. The preponderance of the evidence shows this to be true.

Yet, while recognizing addiction as a physiological, bio-chemical abnormality rather than a psychological problem— because of a lack of methods to treat the disease directly—the disease model of treatment has consisted mainly of strategies for changing beliefs, attitudes, thinking, behavior, and spiritu-ality. These strategies enable addicts to cope with the disease but do not change the addict's physiological and biochemical make-up. These principles have proved effective for thousands of people and enabled many to stay sober who otherwise could not. Without these contributions, attitudes toward addiction and treatment might have remained in the dark ages and in the same category as bloodletting. But these are principles for liv-ing, not treatment for a disease, and do not address the under-lying neurochemical condition that accompanies addiction. They are methods of *coping* with the condition, not for treat-ing it.

This psychological, social and spiritual approach to inter-rupting active addiction works for less than 20 percent of those who receive it. And, understandably, those 20 percent become the spokespersons for this approach to recovery. The belief that it is effective for anyone who truly wants to recov-er and who "works the program" has become the underpin-ning for addiction treatment as most people know it. There is an abundance of treatment programs built upon this founda-tion. The scarcity lies in the availability of treatment for the 80 percent who do not recover and who are then blamed for their own failure. These relapsers believe what they have been told by the 20 percent, that the failure lies in them, not in the treat-ment. *We speak for this silent majority.*

For the 80 percent who relapse, working the conventional program has not enabled them to maintain sobriety. And many, while abstinent, have lived lives of quiet agony, never able to find comfort without the drug that had provided it. For them, pain accompanies the choice to stop using the substance—both during the period of acute withdrawal symptoms and for months, years, even decades into sobriety.

A Word from David: When I first made a sincere commitment to quit drinking, I tried a variety of things to help me. I found that I could not do it with willpower alone, no matter how I tried. I went through an outpatient program at the VA hospital where I received Mellaril (a powerful mood-altering prescription medication) and ping-pong therapy. Not very successful. Not successful at all. I finally agreed to go to an Alcoholics Anonymous meeting. Everyone there was older than I was, and I didn't identify with their "war" stories. So I didn't go back—until I was in danger of losing my family and realized nothing else was working. I went back with a different attitude. And after a few relapses I was able to stay sober. I remember how proud I was when I was recognized at AA for one year of sobriety. What a milestone. But it was a tough year. Even with all the help I had from my AA family I struggled with stress sensitivity, emotional overreaction, cravings, and—long before I had a name for it or a way to describe it—stimulus augmentation.

With Merlene's help I found many ways of coping one day at a time. Nutrition, exercise, plenty of sleep, "escape time," and participation in a church community all helped me hang on and work the program of AA. It was years later, when I started taking amino acid supplements, that I found real relief from abstinence-based symptoms. I am thankful for the freedom that brought into my life. I will be forever grateful to AA because without it I would never have made it to that point. But I understand the pain that leads people back to drinking or using drugs when AA is not enough to heal the broken brain.

Abstinence-Based Symptoms of Addiction

There are painful symptoms of addiction that occur when someone is using, symptoms that motivate the person to give up addictive use. When the pain becomes severe enough, addicted people usually choose recovery. Recovery requires abstinence, but abstinence triggers new symptoms—or the return of old symptoms that preceded the addiction. Some symptoms pass within a few days, but some emerge and grow more severe as acute withdrawal subsides. Long-term and excessive use of addictive substances causes nutrient depletion and tissue/cellular damage that intensify the problems of reward deficiency, which existed before the addictive use began. So when addictive use stops, the symptoms that led to self-medicating with a mood-altering substance return with equal or greater intensity.

The pain of abstinence usually takes various forms: severe anxiety or depression, trouble concentrating and remembering, inability to manage stress, sleep problems, lack of energy, overwhelming cravings and heightened sensitivity to sights, sounds, touch, and pain are the most common.

Stimulus Augmentation

This is one name sometimes used to describe this heightened sensitivity to external and internal stimuli. Sometimes it is referred to as hyper-augmentation, hypersensitivity, or simply augmentation. People with this condition are unable to filter out background noises and happenings and feel bombarded by all that is going on around them. They augment or magnify sounds, sights, touch, pain, perceptions, and stress. They feel constantly overwhelmed by everything going on around them and everything going on inside of them. What would usually be considered mild stress becomes major stress. Sounds that others do not notice are major distractions. Pain is more intense. Being touched can sometimes feel like being mauled. People with this condition feel overwhelmed by a world that comes at them full force.

In most cases, this symptom is genetic. Alcoholics, children of alcoholics, and those suffering with ADHD have all been

Stimulus Augmentation and Alcohol

One researcher who has contributed much to our understanding of stimulus augmentation is Ralph Tarter, director of the Center for Education and Drug Abuse Research (CEDAR). He and his colleagues discovered that alcoholics and children of alcoholics are frequently augmenters (people with stimulus augmentation). But when given alcohol they become what he calls reducers; they no longer magnify input but minimize it. The effect is immediate. The relief is profound. Consequently, is it to be expected that when augmenters discover that alcohol (or cocaine, or whatever the drug) reduces the ongoing, unrelenting noise, stress, pain, and confusion of an overwhelming world, they will use that substance again for relief? Of course! Is it reasonable to expect that they will use it again and again? Sure! If a person finds mood enhancement through the use of addicting drugs, the "synthetic" but nevertheless reinforcing reward will motivate that person to more mood-altering drug use. The self-medicating process that begins with a simple need to feel better can easily lead to addiction and complicate an already vexing problem. But what happens when that person recognizes the need to give up the mood-enhancing substance? The pre-existing augmentation returns along with more intense cravings and the augmented brain begs for relief.

found to magnify perceptual input and this has been associated with craving for alcohol. It exists prior to addiction and probably contributes to the risk that someone will use mood-altering substances at an early age.

Inability to Concentrate

This is a natural result of stimulus augmentation. When the buzzing of a fly demands as much attention as the person talking to you, it is difficult to stay focused on what that person is saying. It is not rudeness; it is not intentional. It is just very difficult to maintain a focus when everything around you is calling to you at the same time. It can be frustrating and embarrassing to realize that someone is talking to you and you have no idea what they just said.

Memory Problems

Problems with memory result from the inability to concentrate. If you didn't hear it or were distracted when it occurred, you won't remember it. Or the memory will be sketchy. You can't recall what was never really recorded in your brain in the first place.

Anxiety

Anxiety is common during recovery. Of course, a certain amount of psychological stress is expected because of so much change going on. Change is stressful, and it is normal to have some fear connected with all the changes necessary to make recovery possible. But stress is exacerbated to the point of anxiety by stimulus augmentation, the inability to concentrate, and memory problems.

Dysphoria

This terms refers to a general feeling of discomfort or unpleasantness. It is the absence of pleasure from the performance of acts that would normally be pleasurable. It can be mild to severe. It is characterized by listlessness and lack of motivation and is sometimes accompanied by hopelessness. Ongoing dysphoria takes the "color" out of life and puts sobriety in jeopardy. Sometimes the dysphoria comes and goes and takes the form of mood swings. Sometimes you feel good and then soon feel very "down." The tendency for you and the people around you is to believe when you are feeling good that you are always going to feel good; it is, then, quite disheartening when you are again overcome by dysphoria.

Craving (Drug Hunger)

Intense cravings, or what some refer to as "drug hunger," is a powerful compulsion to alter one's mood with psychoactive drugs. Stimulus augmentation has been linked to a strong craving for alcohol. And alcohol normalizes it. The sober person experiencing cravings knows what will bring relief. Feeling incomplete or inadequate or unfulfilled is common with abstinence. There is a feeling of emptiness and a yearning for something, anything, to fill up the emptiness. The emptiness begs for self-medication.

The Stress of Sobriety

Stress intensifies all the symptoms of abstinence. And recovery itself is stressful. When you make a commitment to sobriety, everything in your life changes; and change is always stressful. In addition, dealing daily with stimulus augmenta-

Sobriety: Is It Really This Difficult?

I've been sober for a few months, but my brain just feels numb—I don't know how to think or what to think or even if I want to think.

I haven't had a drink in seven weeks, but I feel like I'm going nuts. When my kids yell at each other, I want to curl up into a ball and die. Bright lights, loud noises, intense emotions—I can't be around them. I feel like they are frying my brain.

I'm sober, but my memory is shot, and I'm afraid I have permanent brain damage or maybe even Alzheimer's.

I can't figure it out. I've got eight months of sobriety under my belt, but the anxiety and the fear just don't quit. Once or twice a week I wake up in a sweat, dreaming about the time I ran over my son's bicycle when I was drunk and imagining that I killed him.

Some days I feel great, happy, solidly sober, but then the next day I feel just plain awful. My mood swings are like flash floods—there's never any warning.

I cry all the time. I'm always overreacting to everything—a pile of dirty clothes in the hallway is enough to make me want to scream.

I'm telling you—alcoholism was hell. But what is this, purgatory?

from *Beyond the Influence*[6]

tion, the inability to concentrate, memory problems, mood swings, and cravings creates additional stresses.

In handling stress the brain uses large quantities of neurochemicals. Persistent ongoing stress not only raises the level of stress hormones, but depletes the brain of key neurochemicals, especially the opioids. So during recovery when you are expected to be getting better and better, the stress of abstinence may actually make you feel worse. People tell you to just hang on and things will get better, but they don't. During times of stress the body releases chemicals to help us keep functioning, but the constant excess of these chemicals can cause irritability, sleeplessness, depression, anxiety, and eventually physical illnesses (high blood pressure, heart disease, and gastrointestinal problems, to mention a few), all of which become new stressors.

"Constitutionally Incapable of Rigorous Honesty"

While it offers hope, the book of Alcoholics Anonymous (referred to as "The Big Book"[5]), does state that there are those for which the program doesn't work. It says this is not their fault because they are "constitutionally incapable of being rigorously honest." Well, why would some be constitutionally incapable of being rigorously honest and why would that interfere with a sincere effort to maintain sobriety?

The answer lies in what we call denial. Denial is a mechanism we employ to protect us from a truth too uncomfortable to tolerate. For many addicts the truth of what it takes to maintain abstinence is something too uncomfortable to tolerate. The program of AA requires a person to look squarely at themselves. But for those "constitutionally" incapable of being rigorously honest, denial becomes a wall that will not allow them to look into themselves for fear of the truth they will find. In many people the pain of abstinence becomes so severe that it blocks the ability to do the work of recovery. Sometimes we hear that pain is the great motivator and that is true. Pain does motivate us to do whatever we need to do to get rid of it. It does not motivate us to do what will create more pain (in this case, going through the 12-Step Program). And, when the pain of abstinence is severe and doesn't let up, it is not a motivation to stick with the painful tasks required. Rather, it interferes with the ability to do so.

Consider for a moment that you have a severe or migraine headache. Now consider your reaction if someone were to ask you, at the point of this severe pain, to take a piece of paper and write down your character defects. How capable would you be of doing that while experiencing this pain? But supposing you were somehow able to do that, and, after you did it, you were given another piece of paper and asked to make a list of all the people you have harmed in your life and to state what you are willing to do to make amends to these people. You would probably be constitutionally incapable of doing that. But in some drug treatment programs this is exactly what you are asked to do. *For some people, it is the pain of abstinence that renders them "constitutionally incapable of being rigorously honest."*

These symptoms persist even with participation in recovery activities; and deep inside, the addicted person is always aware of what will provide pain relief. While some people hang on in spite of the discomfort, "white knuckling" it through life, many cannot and eventually give in to the compulsion to drink or take other drugs or to develop a substitute addiction such as gambling or a food addiction.

There currently exists enough scientific data about the biochemical nature of addiction to go beyond treatment methods commonly available. Traditional psychological, spiritual, and behavioral methods are helpful and should not be discarded, but it is time for a marriage between these methods and new strategies that address the addict's physiological needs. It is time to close the gap between what we know and what we do to heal the addicted brain. And that is why we've written this book—to help you do just that.

CHAPTER 4

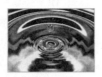

Those Amazing Amino Acids

IN OUR SEARCH for lasting and effective treatment for addiction, by far the most remarkable discovery so far has been amino acid therapy. Neurotransmitters are made from amino acids, the building blocks of protein. Several key neurotransmitters are particularly affected by and involved in addiction. These neurochemicals need to be balanced to their normal state in order for the recovering person to be free of abstinence symptoms including cravings, anxiety, irritability, and depression. Over the last twenty years numerous addiction clinicians have begun treating the brain with certain amino acids that can help restore healthy brain chemistry.

The Brain and Amino Acids

Every living cell is produced in large part from amino acids. Reproducing, altering, or growing any type of cell requires a balance of the various amino acids. Human behavior—cognition, concentration, memory, mood, sleep, thirst, appetite, alertness, and emotions—involves functioning of the whole nervous system. The nervous system is regulated almost entirely by amino acids and their biochemical companions, vitamins and minerals.

As we mentioned earlier, neurotransmitters are produced from *amino acids*. For example, serotonin is produced from L-tryptophan; dopamine and norepinephrine are produced from L-phenylalanine and L-tyrosine; and endorphin and enkephalin levels are increased by D-phenylalanine and glutathione (composed of three amino acids—glutamic acid, glycine, and cysteine).

While it has become obvious that we can nourish an impoverished brain with amino acids, it is not quite as easy as it sounds. This is because the interaction of neurotransmitters is very complex with different amino acids and combinations of amino acids with their corresponding cofactors producing different effects. But it is much more straight-forward therapy than anything most addiction professionals have tried. It is not a gimmick. It isn't a theory. It has been researched and been found effective in the management of addiction recovery. In short, amino acid therapy works.

As we explain in earlier chapters, drug craving and abstinence symptoms are a result of malfunctions of the reward centers of the brain involving the neurotransmitters and the enzymes that control them. We now know, as a result of studies done with amino acids, that it is possible to reduce stress, reduce depression, increase glucose and neurotransmitter receptor sensitivity, and restore proper levels of serotonin, dopamine, enkephalins, taurine, and GABA with amino acid supplementation.[1] If this sounds too good to be true or a dream for the future, let us assure you that it is already happening.

Essential and Non-Essential Amino Acids

Amino acids are the building blocks of proteins, combining into tens of thousands of complex protein or amino acid chains of differing links and complexities called polypeptides. For example, human growth hormone is an amino acid chain comprised of 191 amino acid molecules, while glutathione is a short chain of only three amino acids.

It is generally agreed that twenty amino acids (or twenty-one if you include taurine, which we do) are necessary for protein synthesis. (*Note:* There are over 700 non-protein amino acids which, with the exception of homocysteine, will not be discussed in this book.) Your body is able to produce many of

Table 1: Essential and Non-Essential Amino Acids

ESSENTIAL AMINO ACIDS	NON-ESSENTIAL AMINO ACIDS
Isoleucine	Arginine*
Leucine	Cystine*
Lysine	Glutamine*
Methionine	Glycine
Phenylalanine	Tyrosine*
Threonine	Alanine
Tryptophan	Proline
Valine	Aspartic Acid
Histidine**	Serine
	Cystine
	Taurine*
	Glutamic Acid

* Conditionally essential amino acids
**The amino acid histidine is essential only in children.

these twenty-one amino acids from other amino acids already in the body. Because the body normally manufactures them—and hence they do not have to be in foods we eat or supplements we take—these are called non-essential amino acids. It is important to keep in mind that "non-essential" does not mean these amino acids are not important. It simply means that, under ideal circumstances, it is not essential or necessary to consume them in our food.

But the body does not manufacture all of the amino acids needed in the formation of neurotransmitters. Most are derived from food sources and come to the brain by way of the blood supply. These are called essential amino acids, and, in addition to getting them from the food you eat, they can be taken as individual supplements or a formulated compound, or they can be given intravenously.

Recent scientific evidence has identified an important third category, conditionally essential amino acids. These are amino acids that are nonessential for individuals that are healthy and leading a relatively low-stress lifestyle. But during periods of illness or chronic stress, these amino acids become essential. The body's machinery is simply unable to generate adequate levels; therefore, additional sources are required, from either food or supplementation. Classic examples of conditionally essential amino acids linked with addiction are L-glutamine, L-tyrosine, and taurine.[2]

Most experts agree that there are nine essential amino acids, seven nonessential and five conditionally essential amino acids (see Table 1).

Forms of Amino Acids

Most of the amino acids, except for glycine and taurine, can appear in two forms, the chemical structure of one being the mirror image of the other. These are called the D- and L-forms. The D stands for *dextro* (Latin for *right*) and L for *levo* (Latin for *left*). These designations specify the direction of the rotation of the molecule's structural spiral, as well as which direction light bends when passing through a liquid containing the amino acid. Products containing the L- form by far are more common in nature and are more compatible with human biochemistry. All of the amino acids recommended in this book for the management of addiction are the L- form, with one important exception: D-phenylalanine.

The brain's neurotransmitters are mostly made from the chemical binding of different individual amino acids—with a few exceptions. Some individual amino acids do not have to bind with other amino acids to function as neurotransmitters; they are already neurotransmitters and do not have to be synthesized from other amino acids. Glycine, GABA and taurine are examples of amino acids that are already transmitters.

Amino Acids Related to Addiction

Amino acids that help produce the neurotransmitters most often involved in addiction are:

• D-phenylalanine (increases enkephalin)
• L-phenylalanine (increases dopamine and norepinephrine)
• L-tryptophan, and 5-hydroxy tryptophan (5-HTP) (increase serotonin and melatonin)
• L-tyrosine (increases dopamine and norepinephrine)
• L-glutamine (increases GABA and glutathione)
• GABA (already a neurotransmitter)
• Taurine (already a neurotransmitter)
• L-cysteine (increases levels of glutathione, which in turn increases enkephalin levels).

Read this list again. If you are struggling with abstinence symptoms and/or chronic relapse, it is of utmost importance for you to become familiar with these amino acids and what they do. The more you understand the action of amino acids and the neurotransmitters created from these amino acids, the more ability you will have to manage your own intake and optimize your own brain neurochemistry.

Phenylalanine[3]

L-phenylalanine is an essential amino acid: that is, it must be obtained frequently from the diet in adequate quantities to meet the body's needs. Once in the brain, it can be converted into another amino acid, L-tyrosine, which in turn is used to synthesize (with the help of the cofactor vitamin B6) two key neurotransmitters, dopamine and norepinephrine.

Because of its relationship to the action of the central nervous system, L-phenylalanine can elevate mood, increase confidence and motivation, increase energy, improve alertness and wakefulness, decrease pain, indirectly decrease cravings, aid in memory and learning, and suppress the appetite.

Phenylalanine is available in three different forms: D-, L-, and DL-. (DL- is a combination of D- and L- and can be purchased as DLPA.) The L- form (LPA) is the most common type (found in nature and in food) and is the form in which phenylalanine is incorporated into the body's proteins. D-phenylalanine (DPA) increases the availability of enkephalin by inhibiting an enzyme that breaks down enkephalin, making more of it available at the reward sites in the brain. Enkephalin is a natural, morphine-like pain reliever produced by the brain, spinal cord, and adrenal glands. It helps in the prevention of pain as well, and produces a feeling of pleasure, even euphoria. Enkephalin also reduces stress and maintains motivation. Increased levels of enkephalin moderate or reduce alcohol consumption, while depletion or insufficiency is associated with alcohol addiction, chronic abstinence symptoms, and relapse.

Caution: Do not take L-phenylalanine if you are pregnant or nursing. Do not take it if you suffer from panic attacks or severe anxiety, both of which may be aggravated by adrenaline, derived from L-phenylalanine. Do not take it if you suffer from skin cancer melanoma or phenylketonuria (PKU). Do not use it if you are taking monoamine oxidase (MAO) inhibitors. L-phenylalanine has been reported to cause hypertension in some people.

L-Tryptophan[4]

L-tryptophan increases the production of the neurotransmitters serotonin and melatonin, which reduce cravings and help you relax and sleep. L-tryptophan is not widely available over the counter because in 1988, one batch manufactured in Japan was contaminated and went untested, causing 1,500 people to become ill, resulting in 37 deaths. It was not the L-tryptophan itself that was the problem but a new processing method that resulted in contamination. Unfortunately, sale of L-tryptophan was banned except by prescription. Recently all restrictions have been lifted and it is once again available over the counter. Although it is gradually becoming more available, you may have some difficulty locating a source for L-tyrptophan. If so, you can try the derivative of tryptophan called 5-hydroxitryptophan (5-HTP). Tryptophan is a precursor to 5-HTP, which immediately becomes serotonin, thereby producing the same good feelings as tryptophan.

When tryptophan intake is deficient, serotonin levels drop, causing depression, anxiety, insecurity, irritability, insomnia, and lowered pain threshold. These internal conditions may result in such external behaviors as alcohol/drug abuse, carbohydrate bingeing, hyperactivity, rage, violence, sexual promiscuity, or uncontrolled gambling.

Only a few foods contain high amounts of tryptophan; most foods contain more tyrosine, which competes with tryptophan for entry into the brain. Both tryptophan and 5-HTP are safe and provide benefits as natural relaxants, tranquilizers, antidepressants, and sleep aids. When supplementing with either, it is important to also include B6, an essential cofactor in the conversion of both to serotonin.

L-Tyrosine[5]

L-tyrosine is an amino acid that helps you feel more alert and more energetic. It does this by increasing brain levels of the "excitatory" neurotransmitters dopamine and norepinephrine. It is also an important building block for thyroid hormone. If you need a physical, mental, or emotional lift, tyrosine is the best amino acid to take. If you have any condition that makes it difficult for you to concentrate, try some tyrosine and its cofactor vitamin B6.

L-Glutamine[6]

L-glutamine is an anti-craving amino acid. Whatever you crave—whether it is food, alcohol, or cocaine—glutamine will reduce the craving and help you feel more satisfied and content by directly increasing brain levels of GABA and indirectly increasing levels of enkephalins.

As a bonus, L-glutamine is the primary fuel for the inside lining of the small intestine, rapidly healing a leaky gut while protecting against damage from alcohol, aspirin, and aspirin substitutes like ibuprofen. It is also an important precursor of the body's most powerful detoxifying and antioxidant enzyme, glutathione.

There is a lot of glutamine in uncooked animal protein, but food is not a good source of glutamine; up to 95 percent of the natural L-glutamine is inactivated by heating. The best source is a powdered supplement. It is tasteless and mixes easily with liquid (which should be cool) and is basically nontoxic. However, individuals with liver or kidney failure should not take L-glutamine.

GABA (Gamma Aminobutyric Acid)[7]

GABA is both an amino acid and a neurotransmitter. GABA is the calming amino acid; it alleviates anxiety and provides a mental and physical lift. As stated earlier, glutamine works as an anti-craving substance because it stimulates the production of the neurotransmitter GABA, which is often deficient in alcoholics and benzodiazepine addicts. Although the scientific literature states that GABA does not pass through the blood-brain barrier into the brain very well, reports from recovering addicts suggest otherwise. You can take GABA or you can take L-glutamine to stimulate the production of GABA. Some people take both GABA and L-glutamine.

Taurine[8]

An inhibitory, calming neurotransmitter often found deficient in alcoholics, taurine is normally derived from the metabolism of homocysteine and L-cysteine. During periods of chronic stress or illness, it becomes a conditionally essential amino acid and needs to be supplemented.

Among its many other benefits, taurine acts as a brain, liver, and heart cell antioxidant by scavenging excess free radicals. It also serves as a neurotransmitter, joining with cholesterol to form an important component of bile. It helps regulate intracellular concentrations of magnesium, calcium, potassium, and sodium.

David: I had maintained more than ten years of abstinence from alcoholism when I first heard of amino acid therapy. While I had learned to cope with the discomfort of sobriety I had found nothing that truly gave me relief. I still struggled with stimulus augmentation and stress sensitivity. Another addiction professional told me about an amino acid supplement and suggested I try it. I did, more because he asked me to than because I really expected a positive result. I noticed the effect almost immediately. The major benefit was the reduction in stimulus augmentation. Everything seemed toned down. Life was less "shrill." I felt less bombarded by sounds and things going on around me. In a word, I felt relief. It was as if someone had wrapped me in a soothing blanket. My internal molecules seemed to quiet and slow in their fight against me.

The effect was so dramatic that Merlene noticed it right away. She said I seemed more relaxed and easy to be around. If fact, over time I discovered that any time I failed to take the amino acid supplement she would say, "Did you take your nutrients?" sometimes before even I realized that I had forgotten. I realize now that for the first time in my life I was functioning at a comfort level that seemed to begin in my brain, filter throughout my body, and ultimately affect my behavior. Even though I still have had some ups and downs with mood, this level of comfort became my normal state, and the ups and downs are much easier to deal with.

Some Background on Amino Acid Therapy

One person who has done extensive work with amino acid therapy is our colleague, Julia Ross (author of *The Diet Cure*[9] and *The Mood Cure*[10]), who is director of Recovery Systems in Mill Valley, California. Julia has been using oral amino acid supplementation along with dietary nutrition to modify brain chemistry with tremendous success for seventeen years. We have had the opportunity to spend time with Julia, learn from her experience and expertise, and integrate her knowledge of amino acid therapy with our experience in preventing relapse.

Julia began her use of this therapy, as we did, as a result of hearing about the work of Kenneth Blum in the 1980s. Blum, who had spent many years studying the neurochemistry of addiction, began investigating ways to alter the brain chemistry of addicted people in order to provide them the comfort needed to participate in the entire recovery process. He reasoned that if the interaction of neurotransmitters does not provide a "reward," then craving leads to addiction, which leads to more craving, which, of course interferes with recovery.

After studying the genetics of addiction, Blum took the next logical step—correcting the neurotransmitter abnormalities with the natural substances that produce them, amino acids. He developed the first oral supplement of amino acids formulated specifically for people in recovery.

The following list describes the action of neurotransmitters most often related to addiction, the mood-altering substances that are often used when there is a deficiency, the amino acids that normally produce the neurotransmitters, and the result of a deficiency of each neurotransmitter.

Neurotransmitter: Dopamine
Action: good feelings, satisfaction, comfort, alertness
Substance Use Linked to Deficiency: alcohol, marijuana, cocaine, caffeine, amphetamines, sugar, tobacco
Deficiency Symptoms: "emptiness," lack of pleasure and reward, fatigue, depression, lack of motivation
Amino Acids: L-phenylalanine, L-tyrosine

Neurotransmitter: Norepinephrine
Action: arousal, energy, stimulation, mental focus

Substance Use Linked to Deficiency: cocaine, speed, tobacco, marijuana, alcohol, sugar
Deficiency Symptoms: lack of energy, depression, poor concentration
Amino Acids: L-phenylalanine, L-tyrosine

Neurotransmitter: GABA
Action: calming, relaxation
Substance Use Linked to Deficiency: valium, alcohol, marijuana, tobacco, sugar
Deficiency Symptoms: anxiety, panic, tenseness, insecurity, sleeplessness
Amino Acids: GABA, L-glutamine

Neurotransmitter: Endorphins/Enkephalins
Action: physical and emotional pain relief, pleasure, good feelings, euphoria
Substance Use Linked to Deficiency: heroin, alcohol, marijuana, sugar, chocolate
Deficiency Symptoms: hyper-sensitivity to emotional and physical pain, anhedonia, feeling of incompleteness, craving for comfort or pleasure, craving for certain substances, the "blahs"
Amino Acids: D-phenylalanine, DL-phenylalanine

Neurotransmitter: Serotonin
Action: emotional stability, self-confidence, pain tolerance
Substance Use Linked to Deficiency: alcohol, sugar, chocolate, tobacco, marijuana
Deficiency Symptoms: depression, obsessiveness, compulsiveness, worry, low self-esteem, sleep problems, craving for sweets, irritability, fearfulness, tantrums, violence, promiscuity
Amino Acids: L-tryptophan or 5-HTP

Neurotransmitter: Taurine
Action: calmness, promotion of sleep and digestion, seizure control
Substance Use Linked to Deficiency: benzodiazepines, alcohol
Deficiency Symptoms: proneness to seizures, sleeplessness, anxiety, poor digestion
Amino Acids: taurine

Scientific Studies

In the 1950s, Dr. Roger Williams was a pioneer in the area of alcoholism and nutrition, especially in the use of glutamine. In his research he discovered that 3,000–4,000 mgs of glutamine daily (one well-rounded teaspoon) would stop the craving for alcohol and decrease the craving for sweets.[11]

Through double-blind studies we now know that amino acid supplementation can lower drug hunger (craving), reduce stress, reduce or eliminate withdrawal tremors, reduce cocaine-induced dreams, increase libido, reduce physiological stress, improve behavior, increase focus, increase glucose receptor sensitivity, and restore neurotransmitters such as serotonin, dopamine, enkephalins, taurine and GABA.[1]

Some of the facts established by the studies on an amino acid supplement formulated specifically for alcoholics[1] were that the supplement users experienced significantly less stress, drug craving, depression, irritability, paranoia, anger, and anxiety. They also had more energy, self-confidence, and feelings of well-being. They were six times more likely to complete a twenty-eight day treatment program and had fewer incidents of relapse.

Some of the facts established by the studies on an amino acid supplement formulated for stimulant abusers[1] were that the supplement users had a 50 percent lower drug

Tryptophan for Depression

"Two researchers in England compared the effects of tryptophan and the popular prescription drug Tofranil. (Tofranil, or imipramine, is a commonly used antidepressant.) Both groups of patients with depression improved. The study revealed that tryptophan was just as effective as Tofranil, and there were no side effects from the tryptophan. Conversely, the side effects for the Tofranil group included blurring of vision, dryness of mouth, low blood pressure, urinary retention, heart palpitations, hepatitis, and seizures.

"Tranquilizers provide only temporary relief. We have seen many patients on Xanax that still experience anxiety. They have been told it is not addictive—it is. There is no such thing as a tranquilizer deficiency."

From *Heal with Amino Acids and Nutrients*[12]

hunger/craving score than the control group. They also had a treatment dropout rate of 4.6 percent as compared to 37 percent for the control group, and they also had a relapse rate of 20 percent compared to 87 percent for the control group.

For the carbohydrate bingers,[1] those who took the amino acid supplement for ninety days lost an average of twenty-seven pounds and had a relapse rate of 18 percent. They were compared to a group not taking the supplement that lost an average of ten pounds and had a relapse rate of 82 percent.

In a study published in 1997 two groups of dieters were monitored for two years after they had completed a medically monitored fast. The dieters had used a powdered nutritional drink (Optifast) in place of two or three meals each day. (It is now very well recognized that liquid dieters can lose weight rapidly but soon regain it when they go off the liquid diet. This is because the body has gone into "starvation" mode and when food is available again stores it for future "starvation" periods.) In this study, following completion of the "fast," one of the two groups took a formulation of amino acids each day and the other group did not. At the end of two years the group that took the amino acid formulation showed the following:

- A twofold decrease in percent overweight for both males and females.
- A 70 percent decrease in cravings for females and a 63 percent decrease in cravings for males.
- A 66 percent decrease in binge eating for females and a 41 percent decrease for males.
- Only a 14.7 percent regain of weight lost while the control group regained 41.7 percent of their lost weight.

The Blood-Brain Barrier

Nutrients are carried throughout the body via the bloodstream. As these nutrients pass by, each organ "reaches out" and takes what it needs to maintain itself. Since there are substances in the bloodstream that can injure the brain, it is surrounded by a paper-thin, highly selective, protective membrane that is difficult to penetrate. Certain proteins called transporter or carrier proteins move through the barrier and expedite the passage of select nutrients with a pumping action.

Of course, this mechanism applies to amino acids, both those originating from food and those from supplements. But there's one problem. If too many amino acids seek to cross into the brain at one time, the pump becomes overloaded and only the amino acids in greatest supply are allowed in.

This is why you are advised to take amino acid supplements on an empty stomach—to avoid making them compete for absorption with the amino acids in food. If you take an amino acid supplement with a high-protein meal, the ones you need most may not be the ones to penetrate the blood-brain barrier. It is best to take individual amino acids between meals with small amounts of vitamin B6 and vitamin C to enhance absorption.

If you are taking more than one amino acid, you may want to take them at different times of day. Take L-tyrosine, for instance, when you want to be alert and focused, and take 5-HTP when you want to relax or go to sleep. If you are taking a formulation of amino acids, you may want to supplement the formulation at a different time of day with an amino acid that you are in particular need of.

Oral Amino Acid Therapy

Deficiency of certain amino acids will predispose an individual to the use of stimulant drugs. A deficiency of other amino acids will lead to the use of calming drugs, while other deficiencies will encourage the use of painkillers. Likewise, excessive use of different drugs will cause or intensify different deficiencies (e.g., alcohol abuse results in poor absorption of L-tryptophan from the blood into the brain, resulting in a deficiency of serotonin). The symptoms experienced with abstinence will depend on what conditions existed before the use of addictive substances, what drugs have been used, and how heavily those drugs were used.

Rather than determining which amino acids are appropriate based on what drug has been used, however, it may be more appropriate to determine what effect you get from the drug, and even more on what absinence-based symptoms are experi-

Table 2: Guidelines for Choosing Amino Acids

Abstinence Symptoms	Suggested Amino Acids
anxiety, stress, tension	GABA, taurine, 5-HTP
low energy, apathy	L-tyrosine
poor concentration, poor memory, mental fuzziness	L-tyrosine
hypersensitivity	L-phenylalanine, D-phenylalanine
sleeplessness	L-tryptophan or 5 HTP, GABA, taurine
irritability, negativity, worry	L-tryptophan or 5-HTP
cravings	L-glutamine, GABA, L-tryptophan, 5-HTP
depression, anhedonia	L-tyrosine

enced when the drug is not used. Table 2 offers some helpful guidelines.

The minimum effective starting dose of most of these amino acids is 100 mg per day and can be increased gradually to 3,000 mg per day (except for 5-HTP, which ranges in dosage from 50 to 300 mg per day, and L-glutamine, which ranges in dosage from 250 to 12,000 mg per day) until the desired benefits are observed. Most people respond to daily doses of 500–1500 mg in divided dosages two or three times per day. Amino acids are most effective when taken with water on an empty stomach, especially the larger amino acids (phenylalanine, tryptophan, and 5-HTP) that compete with each other for access into the brain.

If you are on any medication you should only use these amino acids under medical supervision. You should not use them if taking MAO inhibitors or any drugs affecting the particular brain chemicals listed in the table. Always read the labels and never take anything that is contraindicated for any condition you may have.

It is also wise to always take amino acids with a good multivitamin/mineral product. They are important for their individual roles but also because they help the aminos make it to the brain and aid in the conversion of amino acids into neurotransmitters. In creating brain neurotransmitters, amino acids rarely act alone. With the exception of individual, free amino acids that are already neurotransmitters (e.g. taurine and glycine) most other amino acids need the help of vitamins and minerals (cofactors) before the formation can take place. For example, vitamin B6 is needed for the manufacture of dopamine and serotonin, and vitamin C assists in the conversion of dopamine to norepinephrine.

Rebalancing brain chemistry is not just a matter of taking a certain amino acid to produce serotonin, a different one to produce dopamine, or yet another to raise opioid levels. As we have stated previously, neurotransmitters interact in a pattern of stimulation and inhibition to bring about a neurochemical reward. Dopamine has been identified as the primary neurotransmitter associated with addiction, but it never works in isolation. It is the interaction of the various neurotransmitters that brings about a dopamine reward in the limbic system of the brain, and reduces the symptoms of reward deficiency and abstinence. Although a single amino acid may be involved in the formation of a given neurotransmitter, it may require a combination or formulation to correct the problem.

"No drug currently in wide use, medical or recreational, address-es the root cause of neurotransmitter levels. Drugs merely stimulate temporary excessive release of pre-existing neurotransmitter stores. They do not increase production of neurotransmitters. Greater trans-port into the brain of the relevant amino acids, vitamins, and min-erals augment nourishment of the brain when there are less than adequate levels."

Heal With Amino Acids and Nutrients[13]

Supplements that Support Amino Acid Therapy

Amino acid supplements alone are not effective. They need help in the form of other nutrients. Following are the supple-ments that we recommend to provide additional nourishment for the brain or to activate or synergize the amino acids.

Pyridoxal-5-Phosphate is the activated form of vitamin B6. Some people (perhaps deficient in zinc or riboflavin) are unable to activate B6. Pyridoxal-5-phosphate is an important cofactor in the production of dopamine (and hence norepi-nephrine) and serotonin (and hence melatonin).

NADH is a natural chemical in the body capable of pro-foundly stimulating enzymes to manufacture dopamine and, to a lesser degree, serotonin. It has been shown clinically to reverse mild to moderate depression and to help prevent and reverse symptoms of ADHD. In addition, it is a powerful brain-protecting antioxidant.

Folate, or folic acid, is called by many the "miracle vitamin of the 21st century." It lowers homocysteine levels, thereby increasing the production of SAMe and key brain neurotrans-mitters. According to Abram Hoffer, M.D., at very high doses

(5,000 mcgs to 25,000 mcgs daily), folate is a highly effective antidepressant. A more effective form of folate may be methyl folate, its active form in the human body.

Methylcobalamin is the active form of B12. Studies indicate it is much better absorbed orally and a more effective form than the customary cyanocobalamin or hydroxycobalamin.

Magnesium taurate is chelated magnesium (magnesium chemically bound to an amino acid) and is better absorbed and a more effective form of magnesium. Early studies that combined magnesium to taurine indicate a superior ability to control seizures, lower blood pressure, protect the heart, and induce sleep.

Zinc is an important nutrient because a deficiency of the mineral is associated with a myriad of conditions, including those associated with addiction and substance abuse. These conditions include hyperactivity, poor attention span, poor healing from wounds, injuries and infections, chronic diarrhea, anorexia, elevated homocysteine blood levels (hence an increased risk of heart attacks, cancer and strokes, as well as low brain levels of glutathione, SAMe, melatonin, serotonin and norepinephrine), low vitamin A status, learning disorders/impaired learning, poor memory, delinquent behavior, aggression, adrenal insufficiency, immune deficiency, HIV/AIDS, alcoholism (large amount of zinc is lost in urine), and clinical depression.

Safety of Amino Acid Therapy

Since the inception of amino acid therapy in the mid 1980s, thousands of people have taken them safely with few side effects. There have been almost no complaints to the FDA regarding their use. The one exception was the contamination problem with L-tryptophan discussed earlier in the chapter.

Why Food is Not Enough

Since the primary source of amino acids is food, you may be asking if a deficiency cannot be taken care of with diet alone. The answer is "maybe," but not likely. Certainly dietary foods are important, and we will discuss that in another chapter. You can get L-tryptophan from milk to produce serotonin. You can eat meat or eggs for tyrosine to produce dopamine. And these will help you. But diet alone is probably not enough to fix deficiencies—for several reasons.

Modern farming, food processing, and cooking practices result in foods that may not provide the nutrition that our brains need. For example, up to 95 percent of L-glutamine is destroyed by cooking. In addition, there are many people who are food allergic and may not digest and absorb nutrients well. The result is amino acid deficiency. Add to that the fact that you may have a genetic condition, aggravated by addiction and stress, that has created a need for higher levels of amino acids than you can get from diet alone.

There is also a catch-22 in attempting to control craving with diet. In the absence of the addict's drug of choice, there is often a serotonin insufficiency and a resulting overwhelming craving for carbohydrates. Will power alone is usually not adequate to maintain the proper nutritional plan long enough to get the nutrients sufficient to make a difference. Amino acid supplements can offset these cravings rather quickly to support other changes in your diet.

No Magic Bullet

We do not want to give the impression that amino acid therapy is a cure-all. The truth is there is no such thing. While we are enthusiastic fans of amino acid supplementation, it is not a substitute for good nutrition or other aspects of healthful living. (That is why it is called supplementation, not substitution.) Nor do we want you to believe that everyone who takes an amino acid product will get immediate results like I, David, did. Many do and you may also, or you may need to experiment a little. For instance, if you try GABA to relax and help you sleep better, yet don't get the result you are seeking, you can try 5-HTP and taurine instead.

Occasionally people do experience mild side effects or an unusual reaction, such as an upset stomach, especially when large doses of amino acids are involved. In these instances no permanent harm will be done as the aminos leave the body within one to four hours. If this should happen to you and you are taking multiple aminos, stop taking all of them and reintroduce them one by one until you can determine which is causing the problem. Sometimes if the reaction is mild you might want to persist in taking it to see if the effect gradually improves. Frequently the reaction occurs only in the first few days as the body adjusts. The benefits may prove to be well worth the persistence.

Sometimes you may experience undesired results because of taking the wrong amino acid. For example, if you want to quiet your nervous system and you take tyrosine, you will not get the desired response. Finding the right amino acids or combination of amino acids for you is not an exact science and may require some experimentation on your part. Please do not give up if you do not attain the desired response immediately.

An Amino Acid Complex

Often, all some addicts need is one or two specific amino acids to relieve their symptoms and achieve normalcy in their overall mental/emotional state. (And these single amino acid products can be purchased at a pharmacy or a health food store.) But for some individuals, especially recovering addicts who may feel overwhelmed by all they must do in order to stay sober, remembering to take the appropriate amino acid at the right time of day (up to six capsules or tablets daily of each amino acid, two or three at a time) may become more than they can manage. For them, compounded formulations of amino acids make the most sense. Each tablet or capsule contains several amino acids, making it unnecessary to take each one separately.

Compounded amino products are available in different formulations, depending on your problem drug of choice. If you prefer drugs like alcohol and heroin that depress the nervous system, you will choose a formulation developed for those who prefer "downers." Such a formulation will help you relax. If your problem drug was cocaine or methamphetamine, you will choose a formulation developed for people who prefer "uppers"—this formulation of amino acids will provide you a lift and help you be more alert.

Just as it is with individual amino acids, it is best to take an amino acid formulation thirty to sixty minutes before or one to two hours after a meal. Some individuals take a formulation of several different amino acids then supplement additionally and at a different time of the day with the individual amino acid they need most.

Carol, a recovering alcoholic who also has attention deficit disorder, has found that if she takes a formulation of D-phenylalanine, L-tyrosine, L-glutamine, and important vitamin and mineral cofactors three times a day, she still has a down time in the afternoon when she has difficulty concentrating and feels slightly irritable. Some additional tyrosine at those times gives her a lift, improving her mood, alertness, and concentration. Trial and error will probably result in the reward you are seeking.

Guidelines For Amino Acid Supplementation

Here are some guidelines to maximize the benefits of amino acid supplementation and minimize any adverse reactions:

- Take amino acids on an empty stomach, ideally thirty minutes or more before or at least an hour after meals containing protein. Protein is made of amino acids and some of these will compete with and crowd out those you are taking. If you absolutely cannot remember to take the supplements on an empty stomach, increase the dose. They will still help you but not as much as they will if you take them on an empty stomach. An exception to this is tryptophan (or 5-HTP). If you take tryptophan/5-HTP with protein, you will probably not get any benefit from it. Take it alone or with a carbohydrate, no-protein snack.
- If you have sleep problems, don't take tyrosine or phenylalanine after 2 p.m.
- If you become jittery, wired, or "hyper," stop taking tyrosine or phenylalanine. Additionally, take the inhibitory, calming L-glutamine, taurine, or GABA to reverse the effects. If that is not enough, take 5-HTP (always on an empty stomach).
- If you become too relaxed or "spacey," stop taking GABA, taurine, glutamine and/or 5-HTP. Take tyrosine to counteract the effects.
- If you suffer a headache, take chelated magnesium, vitamin B and vitamin C.
- If you don't experience the benefits you are seeking from the appropriate amino acid, gradually increase the dose to the maximum recommended.
- Often SAMe (S-adenosyl methionine, 800 to 1600 mg a day in individual doses) will help your brain better utilize the

aminos. Although it usually begins working within a few days, try it for at least a week because it can take that long to feel the effects. Since SAMe is derived from the proper metabolism of homocysteine, lowering homocysteine with therapeutic levels of vitamins B12 and B6 results in SAMe levels going up.

- If 5-HTP doesn't produce the desired effect, try using L-tryptophan (you can acquire it either through a retail outlet or from your physician).
- Sometimes oral supplements don't work because of absorption or other physical problems. In that case we strongly suggest that you (1) pursue medical care to heal the condition that is interfering with your getting adequate nutrition, (2) read *Mood Cure,* by Julia Ross, for a more in-depth understanding of what may be your problem, and (3) seriously consider bypassing the digestive tract with intravenous amino acid/nutritional therapy, which will be discussed later in this chapter.
- Remember that anyone taking amino acids must take vitamin B6 to properly metabolize them. If you have insufficient levels of vitamin B6, all the amino acids in the world will not produce the amounts of the neurotransmitters your brain yearns for.
- At times when you are under heavy stress, you may want to take more than your normal dose.

Experts do not agree on how long a recovering individual needs to take amino acid supplements. People with less severe addictions may be able to discontinue daily amino acid supplements after a relatively short period of time. But chronic relapsers, those with pre-existing conditions such as attention deficit hyperactivity disorder, and people who continue to be uncomfortable when abstinent need all the help they can get, and probably for their entire lives. This means giving the brain—daily—what it cannot produce naturally with a combination of nutritious food and amino acid supplements.

You might be surprised at how much better you'll feel when taking the appropriate amino acids at the right dosage for you. You will not feel "high." Instead, you will feel happier and less irritable. More calm, rested and alert. In essence, you will feel "normal." In addition, you will notice that you have much less drug and carbohydrate craving.

Intravenous Amino Acid Therapy

Numerous treatment centers in the United States are now using intravenous amino acid vitamin therapy (which we also refer to as IV nutritional therapy), and it is continuously being improved. The intravenous process overcomes some the problems that exist with taking amino acid products by mouth. The effectiveness of the oral supplements is limited to a few hours around the time they are taken, whereas intravenous delivery has an ongoing effect long after the treatment ceases.

Another advantage to the intravenous therapy is that it does not have to go through the gastrointestinal absorption process. People absorb nutrients from the intestinal track in different quantities and at different rates. One person might absorb 98 percent of the amino acids taken by mouth while another absorbs only 8 percent. There is no way to monitor this in order to determine appropriate dosage. So it is impossible to know how much of what goes into the mouth is actually absorbed and utilized by the brain. In addition, addicted people have often damaged their bodies with their alcohol or other drug use to the extent that they have leaky gut syndrome, which means they absorb little of what they consume (and, therefore, absorb little of the amino acids and vitamins they take in). With intravenous delivery, the digestive tract is bypassed, and the body utilizes all the nutrients delivered.

The IV treatment can be used for detoxification or for

enhancing the quality of ongoing recovery. We highly recommend it for those who have a history of relapse.

Intravenous Nutritional Detox

The first few days of intravenous amino acid detoxification may be a little uncomfortable, but nothing like what addicts have experienced with other types of detox. Eric told his counselor when he came for intravenous nutritional detox that he had never made it more than three days in a detox program, despite having tried numerous other methods. People who knew him jokingly called this Eric's three-day syndrome. He said if he was still there on day four it would mean something was working.

The first couple of days Eric was mildly uncomfortable, had trouble sleeping, and was a bit irritable. But it was far from intolerable and he was not thinking of leaving. By day three he was feeling good, sleeping, and was very hopeful that, finally, he had found a way past his inability to maintain sobriety. On day four he told his counselor that his history of three-day-syndrome was indeed "history." Eric had not only made it through the detoxification period, but was already experiencing the clarity of thought that is usually not present with conventional treatment, even at the end of a twenty-eight day program. Following the amino acid therapy, Eric went on to further treatment, which had never been possible before because he had never made it through detoxification.

Eric's symptoms during the first couple of days were far less severe than what is standard with other forms of detox. No matter how effective a treatment program is in helping a person adjust to sobriety and develop the skills for living sober, it can't help a person who finds withdrawal so painful that he or she leaves before ever getting the toxic substance(s) out of the body. Treatment program recovery rates seldom include the people who leave before they complete detoxification. If they did, recovery rates would be miserably low.

In conventional treatment, people go through social or medical detoxification. Social detox generally takes place outside of a medical setting and is done "cold turkey" (no medication). Detoxing cold turkey can be very painful (and also dangerous). Seizures, hallucinations, and even death can occur. (With intravenous amino acid/vitamin detoxification, none of these serious problems is known to have ever occurred.) If a person in a social detox program shows signs of severe distress (such as having a seizure), the patient is taken to a medical facility for medical detoxification.

During medical detoxification, a drug chemically similar to the one being "detoxed," or removed from the body, is given to ease the severity of withdrawal symptoms. The dose is gradually reduced as symptoms subside. For example, Librium or Valium are often used to detox someone from alcohol because these drugs calm the nervous system and allow the body to gradually adjust to the absence of alcohol. During this process the patient can still experience severe discomfort with tremors, nausea, vomiting, and occasionally even delirium tremens (DT's).

Medical detox is much safer than social detox, of course. However, it takes longer than the IV amino acid vitamin process because the addicted person has to also withdraw from the substitute drug. With IV nutritional detoxification no substitute medication is necessary, so the process is faster. Patients treated with intravenous amino acids and vitamins report that withdrawal symptoms are mild enough that there is no need to use any medications.

We should point out that many people who come for intravenous amino acid treatment come as a last resort. They are not addicts in early or middle stage addiction or those who are easy to treat. They may have "failed" at multiple attempts at recovery and are willing to try this therapy, only because they have nothing else to try. They may have lost all hope of being able to attain, let alone maintain, sobriety. We point this out in order to make it clear that intravenous nutritional therapy is not just successful for those who are highly motivated or less sick than people who go through other treatment programs. No, the fact is that in many cases they are sicker, more hopeless, and more difficult to treat—with a long history of relapse as well.

With IV nutritional treatment, patients notice that by day three or four, all craving is gone. This is usually a surprise to them, because craving has been a part of their lives so long that they don't remember what it feels like not to have it. But they are pleased to find that they have no desire for drugs. They feel satisfied and at ease.

Around day four or five, most patients are amazed by the clarity of thought they now possess. With the majority of conventional treatments, fuzzy and unclear thinking is the norm with most people. Clay said, "I felt so mentally sharp [after IV nutritional therapy]. I had never felt like that before. I can think so clearly." Another patient, who had previously experienced some fairly long periods of sobriety with the help of AA, commented that his thinking was clearer after five days than it had been after a year of sobriety in the past. "I feel like I'm starting recovery with my first year behind me," he said.

There is also a dramatic change in appearance, especially in the eyes. People who come to the clinic looking very ill suddenly appear bright and alive. Even people who have had extended periods of sobriety in the past often say they feel better than they have ever felt in their lives.

A commonly asked question is: "How long does it last?" While the experts don't yet know for sure, two key ingredients in the success of intravenous amino acid therapy are already clear. First, those who have been educated about the nature of their addiction fare best; and second, individuals who have developed a self-care plan and a good relapse prevention plan also do best after IV treatment. It is increasingly more evident that people need education about recovery; they need to know the importance of maintaining good nutrition and a healthy lifestyle, and thus, healthy brain chemistry. We know that poor nutrition, the use of nicotine or prescription drugs and even severe stress can reduce the effects of intravenous amino acid therapy. So we highly recommend that following initial treatment, patients take amino acid supplements daily. This helps them maintain the neurochemical balance that has now been restored.

After IV amino acid therapy, patients are better able to do the other work of recovery because their cravings are gone, their minds are clear, and they feel better. Many changes must occur to maintain sobriety, but these changes are very difficult when intense craving, mental confusion and internal discomfort interfere with the ability to make these changes.

Relief from Abstinence Symptoms

Many people who have maintained long-term continuous sobriety—for months or even years—following traditional treatment often struggle with symptoms of impaired brain chemistry—symptoms that never go away. However, these can effectively and quickly be relieved with intravenous nutritional therapy. Thus, IV therapy can improve the quality of life for people who are no longer using drugs but who may not be comfortable in sobriety.

Bob had been sober for twelve years, still attended AA regularly, and thought that his life was as good as it was going to get. He helped others get sober and stay sober through AA, and was grateful for AA and the years of abstinence it had given him. But he was never really comfortable. He was very sensitive to stress and sometimes quite irritable. He also had difficulty concentrating. Mainly he just had a sense of internal discomfort that he could not describe but which never went away. He was not even close to taking a drink but he did want to feel better.

Eventually, Bob met a recovering addict who had received intravenous nutritional treatment, and was amazed that this person could be feeling so good so early in recovery. He began to wonder if it would work for him even though he hadn't had a drink in twelve years. He decided to try it.

Bob immediately experienced relief from the ongoing discomfort that had been with him for so long. Two years later he is still an enthusiastic supporter of the treatment and tells anyone who will listen about a way to feel better, even if they are no longer using drugs.

Sometimes patients feel so good after IV nutritional therapy that they are overconfident about their ability to stay sober. At this point, they have no desire to drink or use, so they believe they never will. But addiction is much more than brain chemistry. It affects all areas of life. Recovering people must also learn new patterns of behavior. Their lives must change. This doesn't happen automatically because of the healing that takes place in the brain.

Often, however, it is difficult for some people who have successfully received IV nutritional treatment to find acceptance right away in a support group. It is difficult for people who have struggled or are still struggling in sobriety to believe that someone can feel as good with only days of sobriety as intravenous amino acid patients often do.

Paul went to his first mutual help meeting shortly after having amino acid treatment. He told the others in the group it was his first meeting and he had two weeks of sobriety. He told them what kind of treatment he had undergone and how good he felt. Not surprisingly, the group was very skeptical, essentially telling Paul, "You are still on the pink cloud. You will come back down. You are in denial." One of the group members then told him he wouldn't last two months. Paul was disappointed in this reaction to what he considered a miracle in his life. But he continued to go to meetings and he continued to feel good. That was several years ago and he has maintained his sobriety despite the negative predictions.

You must remember, too, that for the most part we are talking about chronic relapsers—recovering addicts or alcoholics who have relapsed over and over again with conventional treatment. As we pointed out previously, in many cases the people who come for amino acid treatment are often not seeking treatment for the first, or even the second, time. They are those who have already tried conventional treatment. They are the ones who may not be able to receive treatment anywhere else because they have relapsed so many times before. They are the ones who have given up hope that they will ever be able to find comfortable sober living. Some patients do find comfort and serenity following conventional treatment. But it is for the many who don't that IV nutritional treatment is truly a lifesaving miracle.

A Story of Recovery

Like so many others who find that the road to recovery turns out to be a mountain to climb, Brian was a chronic heroin relapser. He doesn't remember how many times he had been in treatment— sometimes for a few days, a few times for months. One time he went in for detox and four hours later was calling his dealer. One time he stayed sober for two years. One time he stayed sober long enough to get married and have a baby. But when his wife discovered he was using heroin again, she took the baby and left. During his times of sobriety he went to twelve-step meetings and talked about how grateful he was to be clean. He had an outgoing personality and everyone liked him. He seemed to enjoy life.

But Brian had a secret. He never stopped thinking about using heroin. He told himself he only had to make it one day at a time. But every day was a little harder than the one before. He couldn't get rid of the thought that if he could just use heroin once his life would be better. He usually began using in secret and was able to keep anyone from knowing for quite a while. But eventually he would be caught; and back to treatment he would go. Clean again, but not happy, not comfortable. Everyone who had believed in him began to give up on him. He finally gave up on himself and decided there was no point in getting straight if he could never maintain it.

But Brian was fortunate. He had a friend who didn't give up on him. Joe kept encouraging Brian to try again, despite his failures. Joe heard about intravenous nutritional treatment and told Brian about it. It was a hard sell, but Brian agreed to give it a try. What did he have to lose? He felt that his life was over anyway. And deep in his heart he yearned to be able to live a clean and sober life. He had a lot to live for.

As part of treatment Brian developed a plan for ongoing self-care and a plan for changing his behavior if he began regressing toward relapse at any time. After receiving the IV nutritional therapy, Brian felt a relief he had never experienced before. In fact, he felt better than he had even before he began using heroin.

Soon, though, Brian kept waiting for the other shoe to drop. He kept expecting the craving and the yearning for heroin to return, but it didn't. He went to outpatient treatment for some time and it was different from how it had been in the past. He was able to think more clearly and better able to apply what he was learning to his life.

Brian cautiously began to rebuild his life. Even though he had been able to play the role of a happy sober person in the past, this time the difference was noticeable. There was something in Brian's appearance and demeanor that was definitely new and different. He was, for the first time, comfortable without drugs.

Brian still took life one day at a time, but instead of every day being harder than the one before, now each new day was better. He wasn't able to save his marriage, but he was able to become an active parent. In his distant past he had been an artist and began to paint again. He has been clean longer than ever before. But the length of sobriety isn't as important to Brian as is the quality of his life. He feels he is really living now, not just "holding on."

CHAPTER 5

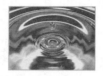

Food for Thought

To THIS POINT, we've had considerable discussion about supplements that will improve the quality of sobriety and help prevent relapse. But supplements are not more important than the food you eat daily. In fact, daily nutrition is one of the most important aspects of recovery. And the more we learn about the relationship of the brain to addiction and of nutrition to the functioning of the brain, the more we know that poor nutrition and problems in sobriety are very much related. In order to achieve and maintain sobriety, you need a nutrition plan based on sound nutrition principles.

Whatever you do to get and stay sober, good nutrition should be a central part of recovery. This includes food as well as supplements. Long-term recovery from addiction requires healthful eating and an adequate supply of amino acids, vitamins, and minerals. Not for a short period of time; not just until you are feeling better; not just until the initial withdrawal and cravings are gone. A person seeking freedom from the

discomfort of addiction must make the same kind of commitment to healthful eating that a diabetic must make. At this
point in time we have no magic bullet to fix either the pancreas
or the brain once and for all. Dysfunction of both takes special
care on a regular basis.

However, we have to admit that good nutrition is a moving
target. Just about the time we think we have it all figured out,
along comes a new study that lets us know that maybe we
don't have all the answers. And then we have to find out if the
new study is valid. Not all studies that come out can be trust-
ed completely. There is often more—or less—to the picture
than we are told. (For instance, many studies are funded by
interest groups that have something to gain or lose by the outcome of that particular study.)

And remember that you have to consider your own situation and weigh the information accordingly. For instance,
many health experts now suggest that one glass of wine a day
may be good for your heart. But this is certainly not the case
if you are a recovering alcoholic. One glass of wine a day may
lead to several glasses, and finally a full blown relapse—certainly not good for your heart. So do not take the information
you read in this book, or get from anywhere else for that matter, as the last word on your health. Keep an open mind and
learn as much as possible about nutrition.

In this chapter we are not going to talk specifically about a
diet to prevent cancer, to strengthen your heart, or to help you
lose weight. You will need to take those things into considera-
tion as you make a nutrition plan for yourself. And there is
plenty of data out there. Instead, we will discuss nutrition
principles that will help heal your brain. Why? Because there
is not a lot of information available about that. A nutrition
plan should be individualized for you by you. Only you know
your particular needs and what will help you stick with your
plan.

One of the first things to consider is that a good nutrition plan should be enjoyable and easy to maintain. Eating is an important part of life that is associated with pleasure. When we think of it as something that restricts us and deprives us, we are not likely to keep doing it. So as we talk about what is good for you in recovery, you need to think about not only how your nutrition can support recovery, but also how enjoyable it will be.

Why Is Nutrition So Important in Recovery?

When your brain is not functioning properly you will feel generally unwell, unhappy and/or anxious. Your stress levels will rise and stimulus augmentation will be heightened. You will not be able to think clearly, and you'll probably not sleep well. And you will begin craving something—anything—to fill the emptiness in your existence. If you want to feel good and enjoy life, you need to adequately feed your brain.

Proper nutrition is essential for a happy and healthy brain. We need protein, carbohydrates, and fat to provide energy, maintain the body, and feed the brain. Vitamins enable the body to properly utilize the protein, carbohydrates, and fat that fuel and maintain the body. Minerals (in addition to building bones and teeth, carrying oxygen to body cells, and maintaining muscle) help vitamins work efficiently. And water performs many functions and is essential to the survival of all cells.

Foods and Mood

In considering how food builds and maintains the body, let's not forget its vital role in altering and maintaining mood.

Depending upon what amino acids they contain, some foods can increase mental alertness, concentration, and energy while others are natural tranquilizers that calm feelings of anxiety and stress. But foods that calm you can also cause you to feel drowsy and mentally sluggish. So what you eat and when you eat it can play an important part in your mood. Let's face it: we self-regulate our mood continually with food. Most of the time, we really don't know what we are doing and go for the quick fix rather than long-term well-being. So for you to maintain sobriety and feel good at the same time, it is imperative that you be familiar with the various types of foods and the nutrients they supply.

Foods for Alertness

As you already know, the neurotransmitter tyrosine is synthesized into dopamine and norepinephrine, increasing energy and alertness. Foods highest in tyrosine are foods derived from animal protein—chicken, turkey, pork, beef, dairy, and eggs. Moderate amounts of tyrosine are found in plant foods such as beans, corn, spinach, oatmeal, nuts, and seeds.

Foods for Relaxation

The neurotransmitter tryptophan synthesized to serotonin promotes relaxation and sleep. Foods high in tryptophan include turkey, green leafy vegetables, dairy products, bananas, pineapple, avocado, soy, lentils, sesame seeds, and pumpkin. There is not an abundance of foods that contain tryptophan and those that do may not contain amounts sufficient to make it past the blood-brain barrier if they are competing with other amino acids, especially tyrosine. However, carbohydrates help carry the tryptophan to the brain. But if you eat a carbohydrate-rich meal early in the day, it can cause

drowsiness. It is better to eat tryptophan-rich foods and carbohydrates in the evening, when you want to relax and prepare for sleep, rather than for breakfast when you want to
become alert and energized. A good bedtime snack is milk and
toast. The bread will help the tryptophan in the milk reach
your brain and, therefore, help you sleep.

Protein, Protein, Protein

A very important thing to know about a diet for recovery is
that protein contains all of the essential amino acids.
Therefore, a high-protein diet will give your brain more of the
amino acids essential for its health. Think protein, protein,
protein. Complete protein foods include meat, poultry, fish,
eggs, and dairy products.

Protein not only feeds your brain and gives you energy, it
also provides the body with the material it needs to replace
worn tissue, fight infection, manufacture hormones and
enzymes, and digest food. The body is damaged by heavy use
of alcohol and other drugs and needs protein for rebuilding.
The body stores very little protein, so you should eat it at least
three times a day. (For more energy and the health of your
brain, we recommend three meals *and* three snacks daily.) You
will probably feel best if your diet contains around 30 percent
protein. Remember that most protein foods are rich in tyrosine.

High-Protein Cautions

Keep in mind that high protein diets do come with some
cautions. Before you go on a diet high in protein, have a physical examination to make sure your kidneys are healthy and
functioning well. Do not go on a high protein diet if you have

any kind of kidney problem. The kidneys are forced to work harder when they have to process protein as opposed to carbohydrates. Another wise course of action when pursuing a high-protein diet is to drink plenty of water. We recommend at least ten cups of water every day, which translates to between five and eight glasses (depending on their size). Adequate water is crucial to protect your kidneys.

Other potential problems exist when it comes to high-protein diets. For one, diets that contain significant amounts of red meat may increase the risk of cancer. Eating red meat, especially fried or grilled, can double your odds of cancer. So, here are some words of advice regarding red meat.

- Eat fish or poultry more often and red meat less often. But even with fish/poultry, think baked or broiled rather than fried.
- Cook meat slowly with lower heat. Try baking or crock pot meals, such as stews. High heat causes carcinogens to form.
- Broil rather than grill. Or microwave before grilling. This reduces the carcinogens produced by grilling.
- Avoid nitrite-cured meats. Most cured cold cuts (and "meats" such as hot dogs and bacon) contain nitrites that can spur formation of carcinogenic nitrosamines.

Red meat is usually high in fat—the bad, saturated fat. A diet high in saturated fat poses many risks, including that of heart disease. A high-protein diet that is also high in harmful fat is not a good idea, regardless of the benefit to your brain chemistry.

Low-Fat, High-Protein Foods

Believe it or not, there are other good sources of animal protein that are not high in fat or that contain beneficial fat.

Poultry and fish are, of course, the well known ones. But most of us easily tire of a steady diet of chicken and fish. Try some alternatives.

Buffalo meat is red meat that is lower in fat than chicken, but still very tasty. If you have a hard time finding it, get a group together and ask your grocer to stock it. Or you can order it yourself by calling Shepherd Farms at 660-261-4567. (Tell Dan and Janet that we told you to call!) We personally vouch for the quality of this source. We know that Shepherd Farms is careful about how their animals are fed and slaughtered, and the meat will come directly from them. We have been buying buffalo from them for about ten years. Buffalo is more expensive than beef, but you are not paying for fat that you don't need or that will cook away. A pound of raw ground buffalo yields a pound of cooked buffalo (or very close to it). Just remember that, because it is low in fat, buffalo can be dry if not cooked properly. We cook roasts slowly in the crock pot, make buffalo meat loaf, and put it in casseroles, stews, and—our favorite—buffalo chili. Wild game also is usually low fat and high in amino acids, so give it a try.

Other sources of low-fat protein high in tyrosine are egg whites, yogurt, feta cheese, and cottage cheese. We scramble eggs with three egg whites to every egg yolk, and add feta cheese and mushrooms—a very tasty dish! Be creative and find ways to enjoy low-fat high tyrosine foods to increase your energy and your ability to concentrate.

Carbohydrates

Carbohydrates are a major energy source and help us use other nutrients. Carbohydrates also help produce serotonin. The "low carb" craze may have you thinking that carbs are bad for you. Like fat, however, there are "good" carbs and "bad" carbs. And you need the good carbs—both for energy and for serotonin production.

When the body digests food, it converts carbohydrates to a type of sugar called *glucose*. As the level of glucose rises in the bloodstream, the pancreas releases insulin, which helps move the glucose into the body's many cells. Once it enters the cells, it is either "burned" for energy or converted to and stored as fat.

When it comes to carbohydrates, there are two types: simple and complex. The biggest difference between the two types is how quickly the body can process them into glucose (simple carbs are processed quickly, while complex carbs are processed at a slower rate). Simple carbs are primarily foods high in sugar (and there are various forms), which include candy, pastries, soda, cookies/crackers, and other sweets, and white-flour foods (including white bread and most of those foods just listed). Complex carbs are found in foods high in whole grains, legumes, some vegetables and nuts.

The problem with simple carbs is that they give you a surge of energy that is soon followed by a "letdown." This occurs because the pancreas releases insulin to deal with the sudden rush of glucose. The body then releases adrenaline to remove the insulin, which, in turn, produces that letdown feeling. Consequently, in an effort to get rid of the "letdown" the body triggers a desire for more glucose (from simple carbs) for another surge of energy. If your blood sugar is low, you may feel moody, fatigued, confused, anxious, and irritable. All your abstinence symptoms are intensified as well. Simple carbohydrates, then, contribute to swings in mood, low energy and cravings.

Complex carbohydrates are also made up of sugars, but the sugar molecules are strung together to form longer, more complex chains, and therefore are absorbed more gradually into the bloodstream. As a result, your brain does not receive the sudden surge of sugar that it gets with simple carbs. Complex carbohydrates provide the body with necessary energy, but without the surge/letdown phenomenon. Complex carbs also provide you a wider array of vitamins and minerals that your body cannot get from a strict high-protein, low-fat diet. A complex carbohydrate snack in the evening with some milk will provide tryptophan to increase serotonin to help you relax and sleep.

Glycemic Know-How: Reducing Surges in Blood-Glucose Levels

Researchers have measured the sugar-spiking ability of specific foods and have given them numerical ratings in two categories. The glycemic index (GI) indicates how rapidly the food is digested, thus how fast it drives up blood sugar. Glycemic load (GL) refers to the ability of one serving of a specific food to raise blood sugar levels. The lower the GI or GL number, the less a food will spike your blood sugar.

Here are a few examples of common foods and their glycemic load rating for one serving:

FOOD	GL	FOOD	GL
Peanuts:	1	Lentils:	5
Grainy breads:	6	Apples:	6
Peanut M&Ms:	6	Baked beans:	7
Microwave popcorn:	8	Ice cream:	8
Oatmeal:	9	White bread:	11
Apple juice:	12	Banana:	13
Coca-Cola:	14	Cake doughnut:	17
Spaghetti, al denté:	18	Sushi:	19
Jelly beans:	22	Corn Flakes:	24
Bagel:	25	Baked potato:	26
Raisins:	28		

The Story of the Potato

The potato is a very paradoxical food. For a while we were told that potatoes were high in starch (sugar) and should be eaten sparingly. At one time the First Lady Roslyn Carter announced that her family was going to start eating better and cut out potatoes. But the potato industry readily responded by telling us it is not the potato but what we put on it that is bad and that potatoes are high in many of the vitamins and minerals we need. Good for us without the bad toppings. So some of us learned to enjoy our potatoes plain, leaving off the butter and sour cream. Recently we have been hit with some bad news again. It is the potato. Researchers are telling us that eating a baked potato is the same as eating a half cup of sugar. Oh, wow! But they aren't telling us the whole story. That is true only if you eat it plain, on an empty stomach, with nothing on it or with it. Butter or sour cream slows the absorption process so it goes into the blood stream more slowly. So perhaps butter and sour cream aren't so bad after all. If you substitute a good fat for butter or use low-fat sour cream, you can get the many nutrients in potatoes without spiking your blood sugar.

It is wise to become familiar with the glycemic load of specific foods because of many misperceptions about which foods are best able to prevent blood sugar swings. For example, notice that raisins have a much higher GL than peanut M&M's. A bagel has a higher GL than ice cream. So while you may think you are eating foods that are healthful and that will help you feel better, they may actually make you feel worse.

In the appendices we have listed some foods with their glycemic index scores. But we do so with a word of caution. You should be aware that glycemic index scores are based on eating these foods alone on an empty stomach. Eating them with other foods will slow the rate that sugar is released into the blood stream. You should not eliminate nutritious foods such as potatoes or carrots from your diet simply because they have a high glycemic index score. In fact, adding butter or sour cream to a baked potato will actually decrease the glycemic index score for the potato. Yes, we know, this is all complex and confusing. The important thing, we believe, is to be moderate and sensible. Try to replace bad fats with good fats as often as possible, bad carbohydrates with good carbohydrates, and so on. If you eat simple carbs once in a while, try to eat them with high-fiber, healthful-fat foods. And eat them late in the day when you want to relax. rather than when you want to be alert.

In addition to eating whole grains and restricting "white" foods, there are some other ways to get the serotonin and nutritional benefits of carbohydrates while keeping a lower glycemic load.

- Eat more legumes (dried beans, lentils and nuts).
- Eat more high-fiber fruits and vegetables.
- Add vinegar or lemon juice to carb-rich dishes; the acid lowers the GI by as much as 30 percent. Eat a green salad with acidic dressing along with carbohydrate foods.
- Eat sourdough bread (lower on the glycemic index than whole grain yeast bread).
- Choose old-fashioned oatmeal over highly processed cereals.
- Eat brown rice, basmati rice and wild rice. (While not actually rice, wild rice is high in fiber, low on the glycemic index, and quite tasty.)
- Eat a bit of protein and/or good fat along with carbohydrates.
- Exercise daily.

Sugar and Other Sweeteners

We have tried to make clear that simple carbohydrates are not the best choice for your diet. However, most people at least occasionally enjoy something that tastes sweet, and you are probably one of those people. If you eat sugar once in a while, do it in moderation. Avoid concentrated sweets such as sugared soft drinks, pies, cake icing, and candy. I eat animal crackers once in a while or a little dark chocolate with nuts. (Dark chocolate is a good antioxidant.) You can also eat foods that are sweetened with substances other than processed sugar. But there are some things you need to consider when you do.

It is very important for you to be aware that honey and molasses are simple carbohydrates and cause essentially the same reaction in your brain as refined sugar. Honey does have trace amounts of vitamins not found in processed sugar and it is also an antioxidant. But it is still a simple carb and will have the same effect on your blood sugar and mood as other simple carbs. If it is a choice between sugar and honey, choose honey. But it is best to avoid both and get your vitamins and antioxidants in other ways.

Many people replace sugar with artificial sweeteners, but there is some controversy as to whether or not some of them are safe. Again, most are better for you than sugar and some of the reports and messages about them have been promoted by the sugar industry. Don't believe everything you hear about them, but it doesn't hurt to be cautious.

Processed fructose is a good choice if you aren't worried about the calories. It does not require insulin to make it available for energy in the body so it does not affect blood sugar levels. It adds the same number of calories as sugar, however, so you don't hear much about it as most people want to avoid excess calories. (Don't make the leap here that all fruit is sweetened with fructose and therefore doesn't affect blood sugar. Different fruits have different sugars; for instance, grapes contain primarily sucrose.)

A good option—and probably one of the safest—if you want to avoid the calories of fructose, is a sweetener marketed under the name of Splenda. It tastes like sugar because it is the chemical mirror image of sugar. That is, it is the L- form of glucose. (Regular table sugar is D-glucose.) The absorption holes in the gut wall are set to allow D-glucose to go through but will not all allow L-glucose to go through. Because it is not absorbed, it produces no energy, has no effect on blood sugar, supplies no calories, and doesn't affect brain chemistry. You only get the taste. It is not an artificial sweetener; it is completely natural and organic.

Complementary Protein

Although it is important to consume the full range of amino acids, it is not necessary to get them all from meat, fish, poultry, and other complete protein foods. In fact, because of their high fat content—as well as the use of antibiotics and other chemicals in the raising of poultry and cattle—most of those foods should be eaten in moderation only.

Because complex carbohydrates (incomplete protein) contain some of the amino acids, you can combine partial protein foods to make complete protein. These foods include grains, legumes, and some leafy green vegetables. Although brown rice and beans are both quite rich in protein, each lacks one or more of the necessary amino acids. However, when you combine beans and brown rice or when you combine either one with any number of other complex carbohydrate foods you form a complete protein that is a high quality substitute for meat. To make a complete protein, combine beans with brown rice, corn, nuts, seeds, or wheat.

As a matter of fact, combinations of almost any grains, nuts, or seeds, and legumes (such as beans, peanuts, peas) will make a complete protein. In addition, cornmeal fortified with the amino acid L-lysine makes a complete protein. A meal of beans and cornbread provides complete protein without meat.

Soy foods are another great protein option. All soy products, such as tofu and soymilk, are complete proteins. They

Legumes: A Great Source of Protein

When was the last time you ate chickpeas, navy beans or black-eyed peas? Legumes are among the most versatile and nutritious foods available. They're good sources of protein and can be a healthy substitute for meat, which has more fat and cholesterol. Legumes are in a class of vegetables that includes beans, peas and lentils. They grow as vines or bushes and develop pods that contain edible seeds. These seeds vary in size, shape and color. You can buy legumes in many forms. For example, green beans are the whole, fresh pods. Lima beans are fresh seeds, and black-eyed peas are examples of dried seeds. Seed sprouts, such as alfalfa sprouts and soybean sprouts, also are considered legumes. Regardless of type, legumes typically are low in fat and high in protein, folate, potassium, iron and magnesium. Legumes also have phytochemicals—a group of compounds that may help prevent chronic diseases such as cardiovascular disease, cancer and diabetes. In addition, they're also a good source of fiber. Peanuts, which are actually legumes rather than nuts, are good sources of protein, fiber, iron, magnesium, phosphorus, zinc, copper, niacin and folate. They're high in fat, although most of the fat is the healthier fat—monounsaturated fat.

contain the essential amino acids plus several other nutrients. Tofu, soy oil, soy flour, soy-based meat substitutes, and other soy foods are healthful ways to complement meatless meals. Another good way of adding protein to meals is to add nuts and seeds to salads and vegetable casseroles. Add protein rich snacks as often as possible. Eat whole grain bread with nut butters or a handful of nuts and seeds.

It's important to remember that plant protein does not provide as much tyrosine as animal sources. If you choose to get your protein by reducing meat intake and consuming more combined carbohydrates, you may want to also include small but regular portions of cottage cheese, skim milk, or eggs to ensure adequate tyrosine intake. Of course, another option is to take a tyrosine supplement product.

Fats

Don't be afraid of fat. Fat provides the most concentrated source of energy, supplies essential fatty acids, and enables the body to absorb certain vitamins. Like carbohydrates, there are what we call "good" fats and "bad" fats. Without enough of the right types of fats, the brain is deprived of critical nutrients and risks falling prey to depression and other mental disorders. The goal is not to lower your fat consumption, but rather to lower your "bad" fat consumption.

Our bodies need fat, and if we don't consume enough fat to give the body the energy it needs, we will most likely crave simple carbs for fuel. An excellent way to relieve cravings for carbohydrates is to eat plenty of good fat.

Fats are composed of building blocks called fatty acids. Essential fatty acids (EFAs) are necessary for human growth and cannot be manufactured in the body so we must get them from diet. Fatty acids can be saturated, monounsaturated, or polyunsaturated. These designations refer to the types of bonds that hold their carbon atom chains together. Another type, trans-fatty acids, is created through hydrogenation.

Saturated fatty acids are the "bad fats" that you should eat sparingly because the liver uses them to manufacture cholesterol, especially LDLs (the bad cholesterol). They are found primarily in fatty meat (beef, veal, lamb, pork, and ham), dairy products (whole milk, cream, and cheese) and tropical oils (palm and coconut). Most saturated fats are solid or semisolid at room temperature. The exceptions are the tropical oils.

Polyunsaturated fatty acids can actually lower your total cholesterol so they are generally good, but at high levels can reduce good cholesterol. So don't overdo it. Oils that contain a high percentage of polyunsaturated fatty acids include vegetable oils such as corn, safflower, sunflower, peanut, cottonseed, soybean, fish, walnut, and flaxseed oil. All polyunsaturated oils are liquid at room temperature and remain liquid in the refrigerator. One type of polyunsaturated fat—omega-3 fatty acids—may be especially beneficial to your health. You'll find omega-3s mainly in fish—particularly in fatty, cold-water fish, such as salmon, mackerel and herring. You can get sufficient omega-3 fatty acids by consuming two to three servings of fish per week.

Monounsaturated fat is good fat. Olive oil and canola oil contain high amounts of monounsaturated fatty acids, 80 and 70 percent respectively. These appear to reduce blood levels of LDLs (the bad cholesterol) without affecting HDLs (the good cholesterol). In addition to olive and canola oils, avocados and most nuts also have high amounts of monounsaturated fat.

Trans-fatty acids—which are very bad—behave in many ways like saturated fat, including raising your LDL (bad) cholesterol. They occur through a process of heating vegetable oil into solids like margarine and shortening (hydrogenating). They are often added to processed foods, allowing them to be shipped in warm, humid weather and left on the grocery shelf for months. Look for the words hydrogenated or partially hydrogenated in the list of ingredients to see if trans fat is included. Trans-fatty acids push both blood fats (LDL and HDL) in the wrong direction. In addition they interfere with the metabolism of essential fatty acids. Canola-based products that offer healthier alternatives to trans-fatty acids are beginning to appear in supermarkets. Make sure that the oil has not been partially hydrogenated.

The following are some suggestions for reducing bad fat and increasing the good:

- Saute with olive oil, water or vegetable broth instead of butter.
- Use olive oil instead of vegetable oil in salad dressings and marinades.
- Use canola oil for baking.
- Sprinkle slivered nuts or sunflower seeds on salads instead of bacon bits.
- Snack on nuts rather than potato chips.
- Try peanut butter or other nut-butters—nonhydrogenated— on celery.
- Add slices of avocado to salads, soups, or sandwiches instead of cheese.
- Try commercial egg replacers when baking.

Vitamins and Minerals

Vitamins enable the body to use the protein, carbohydrates, and fat that fuel the body. Fruits and vegetables are generally the best source of essential vitamins. (However, vitamin B12, without which we develop pernicious anemia, is available only in animal foods. So if you are a vegetarian, make sure you get vitamin B12 in supplement form.)

Minerals are necessary for building healthy bones and teeth, for carrying oxygen to body cells, and for maintaining muscle tone. They also help vitamins work efficiently. Calcium, necessary for building and maintaining bones and teeth, is found primarily in dairy products. Because such foods are characteristically high in fat, you should take special care to get adequate calcium as you reduce fat intake. You can eat low-fat dairy products such as yogurt, skim milk, and low-fat cheeses or get calcium in green leafy vegetables such as broccoli and collard greens.

Water and Fiber

Water is vital to our well-being, in that it helps regulate body temperature, aids in digestion and in elimination of waste, and is essential to the survival of all cells. It also supports chemical metabolic reactions such as those found in the stomach, the intestines, and the blood. Water also assists in the transportation of vitamins and minerals, gases, and waste products. Remember that a high-protein diet calls for lots of water.

Fiber has no nutritive value, but it performs a useful role in digestion. Fiber contributes to good health and provides a feeling of satisfaction when we eat. It increases the feeling of satiation and, therefore, reduces hunger and craving. High-fiber foods require more chewing, causing us to eat slower, and slow eaters usually feel more satisfied. Some high-fiber foods include whole grains, fruits and vegetables, and seeds.

When To Eat

Very simply, you need to eat tyrosine-rich foods when you want to be alert and tryptophan-rich foods when you want to relax. To avoid hunger, eat several times during the day. How often you eat can vary, but it is important not to get hungry. You should eat smaller amounts more often rather than getting hungry and eating the wrong foods. In recovery one of the major things you are trying to accomplish is to avoid cravings. Hunger creates cravings. And when you are really hungry, you will eat whatever is at hand, not necessarily what is best for you.

A nutritious breakfast provides the initial energy we need; it sets us up to function well throughout the day. Sara used to go all day without eating, thinking she was cutting calories. But by dinner. she would grab the fastest and easiest foods she could find, because she was too hungry to take time to cook. Of course, the most convenient foods are typically not the most nutritious or the most satisfying. Once she started eating Sara found it difficult to stop. She ended up eating more than if she had eaten breakfast and lunch. Now that her self-care plan includes regular meals and snacks, she no longer skips meals and has more energy throughout the day. Sara now realizes she was depriving her body of the fuel it needed for her busy life.

Avoiding Trigger Foods

Trigger foods are those that cause you to want to eat more—and more and more. Simple carb foods, like those high in processed sugar and flour, are the most common trigger foods. Complex carbohydrates are less likely to trigger cravings, and it is much easier to eat them in reasonable amounts. Balance, balance, balance is the watchword. Carbohydrate binges are less likely to occur if you balance your carbs with protein rather than trying to eliminate them completely.

If you attend a meeting of Alcoholics Anonymous, you will likely find plenty of coffee, cigarette smoke, and maybe a platter of doughnuts available to all. We know that when alcoholics stop drinking or drug addicts give up their drug of choice, they increase their intake of sugar, caffeine, and nicotine. Why? Because they need something to satisfy the craving created by removing the drug upon which they were dependent.

While this behavior is sometimes encouraged or at least justified with the statement that "eating sweets is better than drinking," in the long run, it is not a good alternative. Of course, for an alcoholic, eating sweets is better than drinking. But the fact is, it does not reduce craving and may make it more difficult to stay sober over the long run. The cravings that continue to plague the abstinent addict is an indication that the underlying problem has not been addressed and rectified. The brain is still crying out for something it is not getting.

How does the brain get what it needs to eliminate cravings and provide a sense of well-being? Remember that a craving is a neurotransmitter problem and neurotransmitters are made from amino acids. So what is the brain crying out for? That's right—proper nutrition.

Sugar, caffeine, and nicotine do not work to rectify the problem. It only seems like they do for a few moments. Like other drugs, they provide temporary relief. But in a very short time the relief is replaced by intensified craving. So they create the same cycle of relief and craving that the drug of choice previously created. And addicts—whatever the type—soon find themselves "addicted" to the substitute.

There are various opinions about the extent to which we should avoid trigger foods. Some people say trigger foods are like alcohol for an alcoholic and should be eliminated entirely, but for most people that is unrealistic. For some of us the sense of deprivation that comes from identifying "forbidden" foods—foods we can *never* eat—creates stronger cravings than eating the foods in moderation.

In truth, there is no simple answer to this. And certainly not one that applies to everyone. But it is important to recognize that nutrition is an important part of recovery and that certain foods can trigger cravings for foods that do not feed our brains. But if you believe that by permanently depriving yourself of certain foods, you risk bingeing on them to relieve the pain of feeling deprived, you should include them in your nutrition plan in a controlled way. Some people allow for a periodic "treat" as part of their nutrition plan to relieve the feeling of an unrelenting deprivation. In order to eat the treat safely, follow a control plan for managing the craving that is triggered.

Sue occasionally gets a small ice cream cone, away from home, and then takes a walk in the park. She takes a small bag of mixed nuts (high in protein) with her to offset the sugar rush. When the ice cream is gone, more is not readily available (since she's at the park), and the exercise helps to relieve the craving. For her, this is much better than eating a bowl of ice cream at home. Ice cream in the freezer continues to call to her until she goes and gets more—and more and more.

When you eat a high-protein diet you will be surprised to find that cravings are greatly reduced, even for carbohydrates. If your tendency is to grab a cookie when you are uncomfortable and find yourself bingeing on sweets, try eating some protein or complex carbohydrates instead of the cookies. You will feel more satisfied and less tempted to go for the ice cream. You will have more energy and feel less anxious. Your brain is getting what it needs to produce the feel-good neurotransmitters that need to be replenished.

Caffeine

Caffeine stimulates the release of neurotransmitters that make you feel energized. In moderation, caffeine will not hurt you. But five or six cups of coffee or bottles of caffeinated soda a day can often cause high anxiety. Caffeine intake has also been

Juicing: The Pro's and Con's

Vegetable juices are not better for you than the vegetables they come from. However, juices are generally healthy and can be convenient. One pint of fresh vegetable juice is nutritionally equivalent to two large salads. So, if you want to drink your salad, that's fine. And you can consume more in juice form. You would probably rather drink six or eight ounces of carrot juice than eat a pound of carrots. If you prefer the convenience of juices, drink them. But, when it comes to fruit, you can consume a large amount of sugar very easily by drinking fruit juice instead of eating it.

Some people like to juice their own fruit and vegetables. But juicing is messy and is likely to be more expensive than eating the fruit and vegetables themselves. The major disadvantage to obtaining your fruit and vegetable in juice form is that you deprive yourself of the fiber needed for proper digestion. So if you're really into a juice program, make sure to eat at least two servings (preferably more) of high-fiber foods daily—such as whole grains, legumes, and raw vegetables and fruits.

There are now supplement products—largely marketed as "whole juice" or something similar—that can be taken as an alternative to fresh juice and fresh fruits/vegetables. Numerous reports and marketing campaigns (most of which, of course, are sponsored by the manufacturers) claim that these capsules are the nutritional equivalent of the fruits and vegetables from which they are derived. While this probably isn't true, they are a decent option if whole fruits and vegetables aren't available.

linked to calcium loss and decreased bone minerals in women. The key word regarding caffeine is definitely moderation.

Weight

Many chemically addicted individuals are either overweight or underweight due to poor eating habits. Proper eating habits will probably correct an underweight problem fairly rapidly. A problem with obesity is not usually as easily corrected. A person can be overweight and still suffer from malnutrition. A weight-reduction program should be undertaken carefully, with the help and advice of a physician.

Immediate weight loss in early sobriety may not be wise because of the physical stress related to dieting. This, along with the various stressors of adjusting to sobriety and a new lifestyle, may be more than you are ready to cope with. Talk to your doctor. It is wise to establish and practice a good nutritional program along with making the other lifestyle adjustments necessary for recovery before thinking of losing weight.

When and if you decide to lose weight, do so sensibly. Beware of rapid weight-loss diets. They can be harmful to your health. Be satisfied with gradual loss. Continue to eat a balanced diet and avoid hunger. Increase your exercise as well as decreasing calories. It is this combination that makes for the most successful weight-loss plan. A focus on good health rather than attaining a certain weight goal usually achieves the best results.

Good nutrition feeds the brain. A properly functioning brain is the key to long-term sobriety. While this is mentioned sometimes in conventional treatment and occasionally in AA, it is seldom emphasized. The role of nutrition cannot be overstated. Addiction is a disease of the brain. Recovery requires feeding—and healing—the brain.

CHAPTER 6

Acupuncture, Acu-Detox and Auriculotherapy

IN THE LAST few years acupuncture and auriculotherapy have been used increasingly to treat substance abuse disorders. Though more research is needed, numerous studies have validated the use of these therapies. Since scientific research shows that addiction, withdrawal, and abstinence-based symptoms are related to chemicals in the brain and spinal cord and stress-regulating hormones in the body, it is reasonable that all therapies that affect these systems be explored in regards to the treatment of addiction.

Acupuncture[1]

Acupuncture dates back thousands of years; many experts estimate at least five thousand years. Yet, in the United States it has only recently begun to be recognized as a valid form of treatment for a variety of health conditions. While many among the conventional medical field are skeptical of acupuncture's abilities, there is strong evidence that it works, especially in the alleviation of pain. It has been used successfully time and again as anesthesia for animals—and placebos don't work with animals.

Traditionally acupuncture healers seek to restore the balance of two complementary energy forces (yin and yang) that travel through the body by way of channels called meridians, crisscrossing the arms, legs, trunk, and head, and coursing deep within the tissues. These energy forces must be in balance for our vital life functions—including physical, emotional, mental, and spiritual states—to operate correctly. The meridians surface at various locations—called "acupuncture points"—on the body, each of which is associated with one or more specific body organs. The idea is that the organs can be influenced by stimulating the corresponding acupuncture point.

Acupuncture involves stimulation of these points on the skin with ultra fine needles that are manipulated manually, and sometimes electrically. It is said that acupuncture moves energy. The ancient explanation for the effectiveness of acupuncture is that when conditions interfere with the energy flow through the meridians, toxins build up in the body and block body systems from functioning optimally. Stimulating acupuncture points releases the flow, and balance is restored.

Western scientists suggest a different or an additional explanation for the effectiveness of this ancient procedure: mobilization of opioids in the reward system of the brain. This theory is supported by the fact that when experimental animals are given naloxone, a chemical that blocks opioids, they do not respond to acupuncture. As stated previously, the opioid neurotransmitters reduce pain even more effectively than narcotics and without the side effects.

There is no tangible evidence of the existence of acupuncture meridians. They cannot be touched or dissected. However, under a microscope the acupuncture points appear to have a greater concentration of nerve endings than other skin locations. And electric skin conductivity, which can be measured, is greater at these points.

Concerning the safety of acupuncture, there is always potential harm when the body is penetrated with a sharp instrument. However, professionals using sterilized needles will seldom do any harm. We advise that you make sure the needles used on you are disposable—the most sure method of preventing transmission of infections, HIV/AIDS, or hepatitis. Most states require acupuncturists to pass a course on infection control and proper handling of equipment.

The FDA has approved the use of acupuncture needles as a medical device. Twenty-one states restrict that right to licensed doctors; the other twenty-nine and Washington, D.C., permit non-physicians who complete a training course and pass a certifying exam.

Specialists in pain management often use acupuncture. If you are recovering and abstaining from mood-altering substances, such as painkillers, acupuncture may be a good alternative for pain relief. Those suffering from back pain, bursitis, osteoarthritis, and headaches can benefit from using acupuncture. In a study in California, eleven women plagued by recurring menstrual cramps were treated with acupuncture once a week. The same number of controls received painkillers. After three months, ten of the acupuncture group had experienced significant relief. The others reported no change.[2]

Acu-Detox (Ear Acupuncture)[3]

About 2,500 years ago it was discovered that the ear contained points that, when manipulated with needles, were effective in relieving the discomfort of withdrawal from opium. In more recent times Hsaing Lai Weng successfully applied electrical stimulation to needles inserted in the ear to relieve opiate withdrawal symptoms. Over several years Michael Smith, a physician at Lincoln Hospital in New York, and his associates refined the detox protocol into five ear points that are manipulated with needles. To promote his protocol, Smith founded the National Acupuncture Detoxification Association (NADA). Currently his protocol is utilized in numerous settings, including drug treatment programs, jails, prisons, and drug courts.

While acu-detox has been found to be very beneficial, you should keep in mind that it is limited to detox from opiate-type drugs such as heroin, methadone, barbiturates and alcohol, but has not been found to be helpful in detox from stimulant drugs such as cocaine. And it is a detox tool, not a tool for addiction treatment or ongoing recovery.

Ear acupuncture is an ancient discipline that has stood the test of time, so even though there is not strong scientific research to show how and why it works, there is plenty of anecdotal evidence to demonstrate its worth. When used in an inpatient detoxification setting, the severity of withdrawal is reduced and seizures can be controlled. It is usually done twice a day in a group setting for forty-five to ninety minutes.

Acupressure

Instead of needling, some acupuncturists apply pressure to the designated points with their fingers or sticklike devices. Michael Smith at Lincoln Hospital uses beads or seeds taped to these points in the ear. He has found this helpful for babies born addicted to crack and for children diagnosed with ADHD.

Needle-less Auricular Therapy (Auriculotherapy)[4]

Although the term *auriculotherapy* is sometimes used to refer to any type of ear therapy, including ear acupuncture, we use it here to describe a non-acupuncture and needle-less procedure that utilizes four cranial nerves and three cervical ganglia distributed throughout the ear, not acupuncture points. It uses a microcurrent device to diagnose and treat these nerves that are a direct portal entry to the brain and spinal cord. All auriculotherapy devices are used to identify the location and measurement of an abnormal nerve point and then to treat that point with micro-amp current at a specific frequency, depending on where the point is located.

The groundwork of auriculotherapy was originated by Dr. Paul Nogier in the 1950s. He discovered that the previously mentioned seven nerves form a microsystem, which is a miniature projection of the body in the ear that represents the entire body.

Nogier first used milli-amp current to intervene at these specific locations on the ear, followed by needles, which did not work as well. Later, other researchers upgraded to micro-amp current, which has worked the best, and is almost imperceptible to the patient. These microcurrents are successful in relieving pain and cause no trauma to the patients.

The practitioner uses a hand-held device to first locate abnormal points of increased skin conductivity on the ear, and then to treat those identified points. The nervous system is tonal, meaning the nerves function at a specific frequency, measured in hertz (Hz). Hertz is defined as cycles per second, or how many times something occurs within a second—its frequency. The seven nerves contained within the ear function primarily at 5 Hz, 10 Hz, or 20 Hz.

Auriculotherapy points manifest, as points of increased skin conductivity, only if there is a problem in the corresponding part of the body which the ear point represents. Once the points have been located, the microcurrent device is used to stimulate the nerve to decrease skin conductivity at that location. The less conductive, the healthier it is until finally when it is really healthy, it is not conductive at all. The point is gone, unlike acupuncture points that never disappear.

Auriculotherapy has its practical application in addiction treatment by causing the specific release of neurotransmitters that may be sluggish or in short supply in the addicted brain and spinal cord. The release of these neurotransmitters is stimulated by the application of specific-frequency microcurrent to the nerves in the ear that directly lead to the brain and spinal cord. The electrical current sends a message to increase the activity of the receptor site so that when the neurotransmitter arrives there and places itself in its receptor, the result will be magnified and enhanced. One reason this therapy is so successful in addiction treatment is that the nerves have direct entry to and from the brain and spinal cord—where the major portion of healing from addiction takes place.

Auriculotherapy is not paint by number. It is always specific to the treatment needs of the individual receiving it. This is made possible because of the precise diagnostic capability of auriculotherapy's microcurrent and specific Hz frequency.

When Paul Nogier first developed auriculotherapy, he was limited to electrical devices that were 9-volt powered, only providing milli-amp current, so it was much less accurate in point location than today because of the inaccuracy of electronics of the age. They didn't have micro-amp current at that point, only milliamp. They didn't have integrated circuits so there were all kinds of limitations. But "auricular medicine" has evolved into a very high clinical degree of accuracy and objectivity in its modern form, auriculotherapy.

Unlike acupuncture points along meridians, points along the nerves are tangible; you can actually see them; you can dissect them; you can measure them; and they have Hz frequency due to the nerve tissue being tonal. Neurophysiology is very tangible.

The auriculotherapy approach to treatment is clearly defined. It is safe and effective, and the microcurrent instrument (model SW-103F) has FDA approval. There are hundreds of diseases that auriculotherapy can diagnose and treat but there are two areas for which it is more successful than any other: pain management and addictive disorders. With pain management it is almost instantaneous; with addiction it is not a "quick fix." But this is where auriculotherapy is a plus. It is useful beyond the detoxification stage. Auriculotherapy is usually done initially in recovery after detox in a minimum of ten treatments in a row, five days a week for the first two weeks. We recommend twenty treatments within the first thirty days, or five times a week.

Auriculotherapy goes beyond the limitations of acu-detox. It can be individualized for each person and for specific drugs, and is a faster procedure as well. When needles are used, they are inserted for forty-five to ninety minutes twice daily. However, needles are inert, do not have frequency or polarity capabilities. Better outcomes can be attained with auriculotherapy in fifteen minutes. With auriculotherapy the skin is not punctured, so it is safer. Dr. Jay Holder and Associates at Exodus Treatment Center in Miami have attained a 93–96 percent retention rate in residential treatment with the inclusion of auriculotherapy.[5] To find an auriculotherapist near you, contact the American College of Addictionology and Compulsive Disorders at 800-490-7714 or 305-535-8803, or www.acacd.com.

Thanks to Dr. Holder for his assistance in writing this chapter.

CHAPTER 7

Chiropractic: Torque Release Technique

DR. JAY HOLDER, Medical Director of Exodus Treatment Center in Miami and Miami Beach, utilizes and teaches the use of subluxation-based chiropractic for the treatment of addiction and, through interview, has furnished much of the information in this chapter. He considers the Torque Release Technique to be the most valuable tool in his treatment "toolbox," along with auriculotherapy. Torque Release Technique is the adjustment of the nervous system to heal abnormalities that interfere with the communication of all systems of the body. To understand how Torque Release Technique works, we need to discuss the functioning of the nervous system as a tonal model.

Speaking generally, there are nine systems in the body—nervous, circulatory, digestive, respiratory, reproductive, musculoskeletal, immune, endocrine, and genito-urinary—but one system controls and coordinates the other eight. It's the nervous system. The primary purpose of the nervous system is to provide communication between every cell, tissue and organ in the body. The nervous system is tonal, meaning the nerves vibrate at a specific frequency. Hertz (Hz) is defined as cycles per second or how many times something occurs within a second—its frequency. These tissues are vibrating at a frequency, pretty much like the strings on a guitar or other musical instrument.

A stringed instrument is an accurate representation of the spinal cord within the vertebral column. Each string is attached to a peg that, if rotated, will tighten the string. The other end of the string is attached to something that's fixed, that doesn't move. We can tune the string to a specific frequency by turning the knob to precisely the frequency that is, say, middle C. However many times the string vibrates back and forth when it's plucked is the frequency. Let's look at middle C. Its frequency is 256 Hz, or cycles, per second. If I tighten the knob, now maybe it's gone up to 300 cycles per second, and it's a higher pitch. This is what we mean by a tonal dynamic. Like the string on a guitar, one end of the spinal cord is fixed and the other is adjustable. And there's a specific tension that regulates the tonal dynamic for the entire nervous system.

Each specialized tissue of the nervous system has its frequency to communicate with the rest of the body. When the nerve tissue is not distorted or under tension in any way, all the different levels of the nervous system are going to operate at their correct frequencies. If there is no interference in the expression of the tonal dynamic within the nervous system, then the different nerve tissues do exactly what they're supposed to.

Each type of nerve tissue is responsible for producing, releasing and/or receiving certain neurotransmitters. When all is functioning well, the frequency is the combination that unlocks the

An FDA First for Chiropractic

The Food & Drug Administration (FDA) has granted a 510K medical device designation to an instrument whose sole purpose is designed to correct the vertebral subluxation. The Integrator, invented and designed by Dr. Jay M. Holder, is chiropractic's first adjusting instrument to apply for an FDA 510K and has gone through an independent, randomized, clinical trial.

The Integrator would never have been invented at all but for the demands required to conduct a human population research study designed by Dr. Holder and Robert Duncan, Ph.D., of the University of Miami School of Medicine.

The purpose of the study—an eighteen-month randomized clinical trial with ninety-eight human subjects, blinded and with placebo control—was conducted to determine the outcomes that subluxation-based chiropractic had in affecting state of well-being (quality of life) in the human population.

Because chemical insult is one of the major causes of subluxations, Holder says that the addicted population best serves as a proving ground for chiropractic. Twenty percent of the American population suffer from addiction. Up to 83 percent of all crime is drug-related. By error of omission, the nation's leading cause of death is drug-related. And the addicted population is identified as suffering from a lack of well-being or inabilit to maintain a quality of life equal to the rest of the general population.

[The study's] results assessed by Dr. Duncan revealed a retention rate of 100 percent, a significant reduction in nursing station visits, and improvements in depression and anxiety compared to results typically achieved in one year of standard medical model (versus only four weeks of chiropractic therapy).

Adapted from the *Chiropractic Journal*, March 1997

tissue to endogenous release and reception of these neurotransmitters, and the individual is at his or her optimal function and state of well-being. This is all based on the structures of the body functioning without interference. Structure governs function. A subluxation is a disruption within the nervous system that interrupts the flow of communication from the nervous system to other systems of the body.

Let's use another example to explain a subluxation. Let's say you have your car radio tuned to 99.1 on your FM radio dial (the frequency), and you're listening to the news. All of a sudden you hit a bump, and the tuning knob rotates to the right or to the left just a fraction of a millimeter; instead of being at 99.1, you're now at 99.100002, about a hair of a rotation in the knob. Despite it being a very slight adjustment in the frequency, you suddenly can't hear the news very well, or you may not be able to hear it at all.

In simple terms, a subluxation is a disturbance to the frequency of the nervous system, most likely caused by the inability of the vertebrae to move properly. Subluxations can result from conditions or events that "insult" the nervous system, causing the vertebrae to "shift" improperly. These conditions/events include physical trauma, such as from a fall or an accident, mental stress, contaminants in the air you breathe, excessive dieting, anorexia, bulimia, poor eating habits, genetic or prenatal conditions, food allergies, and food sensitivities.

Of course, the causes of subluxation most relevant to individuals recovering from addiction include alcohol, cocaine, heroin, nicotine, and legal over-the-counter and prescription drugs. Chemicals cause subluxations, no matter how they get into your body, whether you're breathing them, using them illegally or recreationally, or following your doctor's advice and using an OTC drug or prescription drug. The nervous system doesn't play favorites here. Any of these chemicals

New Technique Introduced; EEG Confirms Results

Lasca Hospers, D.C., Ph.D., a renowned neuroscientist in EEG, was intrigued by the concept and application of a new technique that integrated the new scientific principles of quantum physics, right brain processing (mind/body) and the original principles of chiropractic.

In an auditorium packed to capacity, Dr. Hospers stood up and challenged [Dr. Jay] Holder to an on-the-spot test. "I'll bring in our equipment and run an EEG, then have you adjust the patient with your new instrument and technique and then run another EEG to compare the difference," said Hospers, who is a prominent expert in the brain mapping of patients suffering from attention deficit hyperactivity disorder (ADHD).

For the challenge, Hospers chose a person known to have ADHD. Hospers knew that the person she chose would have abnormal prefrontal spiking on EEG and the pre-adjustment strip confirmed that prediction, which is typical in ADHD patients.

Holder then checked the patient by using the Torque Release Technique methodology and adjusted with a new hand-held instrument prototype called the Integrator. After the patient was adjusted, a post EEG was run and examined. Hospers explained her findings: "All of the abnormal prefrontal spiking found earlier was gone and the entire EEG was now essentially normal."

*International Chiropractors Association
of California Journal*, May 1996
Also reported in *Science*, March/April 1995

can create neurological insult, or subluxation, which ultimately interferes with the release of and reception of (at recepter sites) proper neurotransmitters.

Torque Release Technique is a chiropractic technique that allows for locating and diagnosing the subluxation in the vertabrae, and then making proper adjustments that allow for the proper functioning of the nervous system. There are many techniques in chiropractic, but Torque Release Technique is the only one that has been proven in randomized clinical trials to be effective in the treatment of addiction. In the studies, Torque Release Technique demonstrated a 100-percent retention rate in a 30-day residential addiction treatment model. It has also shown statistically significant improvement in outcomes of depression and anxiety.[1]

Torque Release Technique does not treat addiction directly. Instead, it removes interference in the communication system of the body by directing itself to meeting the needs of the tonal model of the nervous system, whatever those needs may be. In essence, by correcting the subluxation state, Torque Release Technique can allow the nervous system to be free from interference so that it can use other healing interventions to their greatest advantage.

And if this happens, then the individual will be able to utilize amino acid therapy, acupuncture, biofeedback, group therapy/counseling, or essential oil therapy more effectively. Lowering anxiety and depression will allow the addict to embrace the treatment strategies that support long-term recovery.

Consequently, Torque Release Technique is not a substitute for nutritional and amino acid therapy, counseling, or group therapy. If you have an automobile with a great electrical system, but the gas tank is empty, it won't take you anywhere. Conversely, if there is a disruption in the the car's electrical system, despite having the highest quality fuel, the car will also be useless. The same is true of the body. You need a wiring system that works well, and you need the right fuel. One is not secondary to the other. They are each important, and they're only as good as their relationship to each other.[2]

Torque Release Technique is performed with a hand-held instrument, called "The Integrator"—invented and developed for that purpose by Dr. Holder. Dr. Holder recommends using the Integrator[3], the first device found to be safe and effective by the FDA, for the correction of the vertebral subluxation (see sidebars). The speed of the Integrator is one ten-thousandth of a second, providing greater force with a lighter touch, which makes it safer.

Some people ask why they hear no popping sounds—which they associate with chiropractic manipulation—when receiving Torque Release Technique. It is because this technique does not involve physical movement of the bones or joints. It is a neurological intervention, not an orthopedic procedure or adjustment. Those who provide Torque Release Technique claim that within seconds, all the various parts of the nervous system can be set on the right channel, thus allowing the body's cells to receive the messages they're supposed to receive.

To find a chiropractor trained in Torque Release Technique in your area, contact the Holder Research Institute at 800-490-7714 or 305-535-8803, or visit www.torquerelease.com.

CHAPTER 8

Brainwave Biofeedback (Neurofeedback)

THE NERVOUS SYSTEM has two major components—voluntary and involuntary. The voluntary component is totally under your control. If you want to move your leg or arm, you simply decide to do it, and your brain does the rest. It sends a message via the nerves down to the leg, and the leg moves. By contrast, the involuntary nervous system that controls such body functions as heart rate, blood pressure, and skin temperature operates out of its own conscious awareness and without conscious direction from you. However, you can learn *how* to control, or at least affect, many of the involuntary mechanisms, including muscle tension, heart rate, blood supply to the skin, and even your emotions.

Biofeedback is a process by which you learn to recognize signals your body provides that tell you how it is functioning. When you take your heart rate, your temperature, your blood pressure, or weigh yourself, you are receiving a form of feedback from your body about your body.

Do you remember the mood rings that were popular a number of years ago? The ones that that changed colors according to your mood? These rings provide a form of biofeedback, changing color as your body temperature changes.

Thermometers are another biofeedback tool. As your temperature goes up or down, the thermometer provides feedback in the form of the mercury going up or down (or as is the case nowadays, changing numbers in the digital display). Mood rings and thermometers are real examples of how we can have some control over "involuntary" body functions such as blood pressure, heart rate, and temperature, by utilizing biofeedback.

No matter what type of biofeedback we receive, the more feedback we get, the better we can control "involuntary" functions on demand.

Neurofeedback

Neurofeedback (also called *brainwave biofeedback* and *EEG biofeedback*) is a technique by which you teach, or train, your brain to regulate itself. Neurofeedback allows you to consciously change your mental states by helping you learn to increase or decrease the frequency of your brainwaves. It involves displaying a person's brainwaves on a computer screen and helping that person learn to control them.

Neurofeedback serves a dual role. First, brainwaves displayed on a computer monitor can identify a brain that is not functioning well. With the same technology it is possible to control the brainwaves and enable the brain to function better. You can challenge the brain to function better just as, with exercise, you can challenge your muscles to function better.

The procedure, which is noninvasive, is also quite simple.

Electrodes are attached to the scalp in order to monitor brainwaves. These electrodes are connected to a computer that supplies feedback as to what is occurring in the brain. Frequency is the rate at which electrical charges move through brain cells. The human brain is measured by four basic frequency ranges:

- Delta, the sleep state: very slow brainwaves; just four cycles per second, or four hertz (Hz).
- Theta, a deeply relaxed, daydreaming state, 4 to 8 Hz.
- Alpha, a relaxed but alert state at 8 to 13 Hz.
- Beta: the most rapid brainwaves, reflecting normal waking consciousness in a range from 12 to 35 Hz (a relaxed but alert state of low beta is 12 to 15 Hz, mid-range beta is 15 to 19 Hz, an excited, hyper state of high beta can be as high as 35 Hz).

It seems that problems occur when the speed of the brain's waves is either too slow or too fast. There is speculation that brainwave frequency may be a major component in a multitude of disorders. Of course, the goal of neurofeedback is to stabilize brainwave frequency.

Dale Walters, a friend and colleague who worked extensively with neurofeedback at the Menninger Clinic, first introduced us to it for use with attention deficit hyperactivity disorder and addiction. Kathy Sloan, with whom we have worked in her wellness clinic, has used it very successfully to treat ADHD, addiction and other brain disorders. It is now being used for closed head injury, post-traumatic stress disorder, seizures, sleep disorders, depression, and Tourette syndrome. And it can be used by anyone to promote relaxation and a sense of well-being, and to enhance alertness as well.

Training Your Brain with Neurofeedback

Two things happen with neurofeedback training. First, you can learn self-regulation; that is, learn to alter your own brainwaves. You can learn how to speed up the frequency when you need to concentrate and to slow the frequency when you need to relax. Like other types of biofeedback, neurofeedback provides access to our internal processes and allows us to regulate them. The reward of successful self-regulation is the ability to relax if you are highly stressed or the ability to focus your attention if you have trouble concentrating.

Second, with neurofeedback training, actual changes occur in the brain. People who use brain mapping or brain scans report that as a result of neurofeedback, changes take place in the electrical activity of the brain; and these changes persist long term. (It's important to know that medication can normalize brainwaves only while it is in your system.) Deep probes in animal brains have shown that the training has produced actual changes in the brain's neurons.[1] A ten-year study by Joel Lubar and Associates[2] showed that neurofeedback can effectively change what drugs and therapy often can't.

Brainwaves are reflective of underlying conditions, an expression of neurotransmitter activity. According to Lubar, receiving neurofeedback increases the blood flow to the brain. Blood flow, metabolism, and high-frequency electrical activity all work together to help the brain reset itself in a normal range. When brainwaves are stabilized, symptoms are brought under control. When the problem is slow brainwaves and feedback enables the participant to increase beta frequency, he or she is then better able to concentrate. When feedback is used to reduce depression, the person can take more responsibility and function better. When the problem is substance use, the desire for the substance diminishes.

Neurofeedback sessions are actually fun and simple for both children and adults. It is like playing video games; however, instead of controlling the game with your hands, you control the activity with your mind. Each time the brainwaves find their way into the optimal state set by the practitioner, participants are rewarded with positive feedback. This might be in the form of a Pac Man gobbling up his enemy, a car accelerating, or a pleasant tone or image on the computer monitor. Or participants may make a circle or bar grow. The practitioner sets parameters to be challenging but not too difficult, so that participants can move slowly into their optimal brain states. As they learn to control the signals, they are controlling their own brainwave patterns. Just like a video game or physical performance, you start at a level that is fairly easy and gradually increase the challenge as your skills increase.

One of the great advantages of neurofeedback over some other neurological interventions is that it can be tailored to each individual. Brainwaves can be mapped and analyzed for deviations from the norm. For instance, if there is too much theta—which often occurs in brain trauma, depression, and ADHD—and not enough beta, the practitioner will set parameters to increase beta. After approximately 20 sessions, the brain becomes able to find the optimal state on its own without the help of feedback.

One of the pioneers of neurofeedback was Barry Sterman, professor of neurobiology and biobehavioral psychiatry at the UCLA School of Medicine, who in the 1970s used a kind of beta wave called sensory motor rhythm (SMR), in the 12 to 15 Hz range, to treat epilepsy.[3] His original work was on animals. He found that cats and monkeys could be trained to control their brainwaves.

After Sterman achieved a 60 percent success rate with humans who had even the most severe form of epilepsy, experiments were done at other institutions with even higher success rates.

Beta Training[4]

One of Sterman's researchers, Joel Lubar of the University of Tennessee at Knoxville, noticed that hyperactivity decreased in patients treated for epilepsy and, based on this, created the protocol now used for treatment of ADHD. The protocol for people with ADHD is called "beta training" because ADHD sufferers often show a brainwave pattern that is recognizably different from "normal" in that there is an excess of theta waves (associated with a daydreaming state) and a deficit of beta waves (associated with focus and attention). It makes sense, then, that individuals with ADHD are more detached and less focused. With neurofeedback those with ADHD learn to inhibit their theta waves and enhance their beta waves. It has been regularly demonstrated that with twenty to thirty sessions, people with ADHD can learn to experience greater clarity of thought and higher energy levels. Over time these changes have been shown to continue even without further treatments. Joel Lubar claims that more than 90 percent of his patients have benefited.

Alpha-Theta Protocol[16]

The alpha-theta protocol is very different from beta training. It takes place in the lower registers of the brain's frequencies. The first study of the effectiveness of the alpha-theta protocol on substance abusers was begun in 1982 by Eugene Peniston, a researcher at the Sam Rayburn Memorial Veterans' Center in Bonham, Texas. Peniston hypothesized that alcoholics drink because they cannot get into alpha states naturally, and consequently cannot produce soothing neurotransmitters on their own. He compared ten alcoholics treated with traditional counseling with ten others who had the same counseling plus the alpha-theta training. Peniston claims an 80 per-

"It Was As If Someone Had Flipped A Switch"

Beta training was where I started my journey with neurofeedback. I was curious about the technology. For a half hour or so, I watched a game: white lines formed in the middle of the highway and a beep sounded when I produced the right brainwaves. About an hour after that, it was as if someone had flipped a switch. The world looked sharp and crystalline, its colors richer. My thinking was sharper and I had a quiet kind of energy. It lasted a couple of hours.

After five or six sessions, the God-just-painted-the-world effect dissipated, but I noticed other changes. I felt calmer and more centered. I felt more secure in social situations. Particularly important to me was that my mornings were much more productive. I always drink coffee and drag my tail until late morning. Lately I've been getting up, ready to go. By the fifteenth session, the change was unmistakable. As of this writing, it has lasted about a month.

Jim Robbins[5]

cent success rate with the group who used the neurofeedback—compared to only 20 percent for those receiving traditional treatment.

Memory Training

Scientists from Imperial College, London, and Charing Cross Hospital have announced[7] that they have been able to improve working memory by 10 percent with neurofeedback training. The term "working memory" refers to the type of memory used to hold and then apply information to perform a task, such as "recording" a phone number in your mind in order to recall and use it later. This is good news for people in recovery with memory problems.

We should note here that neurofeedback is not a method for detoxification. You should have completed withdrawal before using it. We would also caution you to work with a practitioner who identifies your specific brainwave patterns to determine the type of protocol most appropriate for you.

There are critics of neurofeedback who say that any benefits are due to a placebo effect, but animal studies show that placebo cannot be the primary reason that brainwave biofeedback is effective. Why is this important? Simple—*placebos do not work on animals.*

Of course, there is always the possibility of placebo effects in human studies. Expectancy does produce a reaction. But the practitioner can alternate protocols and get different results. (False feedback does not produce the same effect as accurate feedback.) This would not be the case with a placebo effect. Because the participant is not able to tell when the practitioner switches protocols, he or she would not respond because of expectation.

Whether you have a specific disorder, such as ADHD, or just want to improve the functioning of your brain, neurofeedback can be beneficial. When your brain performs better, you will sleep better, you will feel more serene, you will be able to manage your focus and attention, and you will feel more emotionally stable.

Thanks to Dr. Joel Lubar for his contributions to this chapter. For more information on Dr. Lubar and his research, refer to his website, www.eegfeedback.org.

CHAPTER 9

Body Work

THERE ARE A variety of body therapies that you might find beneficial in recovery for natural pain relief, relieving stress, increasing energy, and lifting your mood. Many of these touch therapies are becoming more and more popular as the benefits become better known. Any of the following methods of balancing or relaxing body tissue can enhance comfort in sobriety.

Therapeutic Massage

Therapeutic massage is used for both relieving pain and reducing stress. In fact, it is based on the idea that there is a relationship between muscle pain and stress. That is, relaxing muscles reduces stress and reducing stress relaxes muscles. The added benefit is that when stress responses are lowered, physical disorders such as high blood pressure and diabetes improve.

Therapeutic massage originated about five thousand years ago in Sweden, and is sometimes referred to as Swedish massage, thus having passed the test of time as a means of improving health and well-being.

Reiki and Therapeutic Touch

Reiki and *therapeutic touch* are techniques concerned with moving energy through the body to restore balance. They are based on the idea that there are energy fields within and around the body. These techniques are intended to balance and restore harmony throughout the energy system of the body.

Reiki originated in Japan as a way to bring the mind, body, and spirit into balance. It came from a technique described in Tibetan scriptures almost three thousand years ago. Therapeutic touch is the work of Dora Kuntz and Delores Krieger influenced by the practices of yoga, ayurvedic, Tibetan, and Chinese health systems.

With both techniques, there may or may not be actual physical touch between the therapist and the client although Reiki is usually a hands-on procedure and therapeutic touch is usually hands off. Therapeutic touch is usually done with the hand about four inches or so above the body. It is sometimes said that Reiki allows the energy flow and therapeutic touch directs the energy flow.

Therapeutic touch includes an assessment during which the therapist identifies blocks in energy flow by a feeling of coldness, infections or excess energy by a feeling of warmth, and congestion by a variation in the sensations experienced. The practitioner works with the client until these areas all feel similar; i.e., no area is hotter, colder, or more congested than another. The average treatment lasts about twenty minutes.

Research has discovered that the benefits of Reiki and therapeutic touch are similar: relaxation, decreased anxiety, increased sense of well-being, and healing. Both have been found to induce a calming effect and to decrease anxiety. The need for pain medications has been found to be less when therapeutic touch is used by nurses.

For more information about therapeutic touch, call 703-437-4377. For more information about Reiki, call the International Center for Reiki Training at 800-332-8112.

Reflexology

Reflexology is a micro-system therapy; that is, various points on the feet are thought to represent various organs and parts of the body. Reflexologists claim that work on these points improves blood flow and energy, thus improving functioning in that part of the body. Tenderness at a specific site on the foot indicates a potential problem to that associated part of the body. Pressure on that spot leads to unblocked energy.

During a reflexology session, the therapist applies gentle but firm pressure or massage to your feet. Like a good massage, reflexology is very relaxing and is said to lessen anxiety. It is generally safe, but there are still some precautions you should take. For example, if your feet have been injured in any way, postpone treatment until they've healed. Most reflexologists will not treat you if you have a fever, after recent surgery, if you have clots in the veins, ulcers, or any other vascular problem in your lower legs, or if you have a pacemaker. So long as these precautions are followed and reflexology is not relied on for any diagnostic purposes, it appears to be a safe way to decrease tension and give some relief of pain. For more information, call the International Institute of Reflexology at 813-343-4811.

Rolfing

Rolfing, developed by a biophysicist named Ida Rolf, focuses on the fascia, or connective tissue, which binds and connects the body's bones and muscles. Normal fascia is loose, moist, and mobile, allowing muscles and joints to move easily and remain flexible. Chronic stress, injury, and inactivity cause the fascia to thicken and its layers to become fused together.

The purpose of Rolfing is to stretch and unwind the thickened fascia, reestablish proper alignment, restore the normal relationship between bones and muscles, and improve their function. Rolfers claim to be able to reduce pain and spasm, raise energy levels, improve mood, and leave the body more limber, with increased range of motion in the joints. For more information on Rolfing, contact the Rolf Institute of Structural Integration at 800-530-8875.

Myofascial Release

As the name implies, myofascial release also focuses on the connective tissue of the body. It is based on the idea that when this myofascia is damaged, the constrictions and restrictions interfere with proper functioning throughout the body. When these constrictions are released, there is not only physical relief but also emotional and mental release. Although there are few studies to support this therapy, it is rapidly becoming more popular, and many who experience it report dramatic outcomes. For more information about this therapy, contact Myofascial Release Treatment Centers at 1-800-FASCIAL.

Merlene: Because my daughter-in-law is a massage therapist that practices myofascial release, I had heard quite a bit about its benefits and many stories of astounding outcomes. I had her give me a couple of massages, and then decided to get what is called an "intensive," about 100 hours in three weeks time, from a therapist in my area. It was an amazing experience.

There is something that happens with MFR that I have not heard about with other forms of massage. That is involuntary movement. The therapist massages one part of the body, and there is movement in another part. I don't mean this is involuntary movement in the sense that I couldn't stop it but in the sense that I didn't consciously initiate it. And I usually did not attempt to stop it because I did not feel at risk in any way. If I did, I could have stopped it. Sometimes it felt as if I had large strands of taffy inside and someone was pulling the taffy on one end causing a response at the point where it was connected at the other end.

After I was comfortable with what was happening to me I was able to relax and just let it happen, often entering a very relaxed state in which I had a sense of enlightenment and awareness. At the end of my "intensive" I felt better physically, mentally, and spiritually than I can remember feeling since I was a child. I had much more freedom of movement; I felt clean mentally and emotionally, and my energy level was much increased.

The Rosen Method

The Rosen Method is a therapy developed by Martha Rosen that combines massage with a form of nondirective counseling. It is based on the idea that traumas and memories are stored in the body as muscular tension. Agitated emotions often result in tense muscles, and those emotions can be released through massage. As the massage moves to various areas of the body the therapist—while monitoring breathing and asking questions—gets the client to talk about potentially emotional blocks. The combination of massage and discussion can bring memories and emotions to the surface. Often, awareness of the emotion is therapeutic and in other instances talking about the emotions is helpful. For more information, contact the Rosen Institute at 510-845-6606.

Shiatsu

This therapy originated in Japan about seventy years ago, and is based on Chinese medicine practice. It is considered massage, but is really more a form of acupressure. It targets the same points as acupuncture, where energy flows along meridians throughout the body. It is credited with bringing about the same types of results as acupuncture, primarily pain relief and relaxation.

Craniosacral Therapy

Cerebrospinal fluid bathes the brain and the tissues of the spinal cord. It is prevented from leaking out into the rest of the body by a membrane that encloses the entire nervous system. Cerebrospinal fluid normally flows freely from the head (cranium) to the base of the spine (sacrum). According to craniosacral therapists, this nervous system circulation has a rhythm of its own. They theorize that anything that interrupts the normal flow of cerebrospinal fluid or alters its rhythm and pressure can cause physical and mental problems.

William Sutherland, an osteopath, formulated the theory of craniosacral therapy in the early 1900s. During the last twenty years, his work has been continued and popularized by another osteopathic physician, John Upledger. In the late 1970s, Upledger headed a team of scientists at Michigan State University that produced a model demonstrating the movement of fluid in the nervous system from the head to the sacrum (tailbone). They concluded that the craniosacral system acts like a semi-closed hydraulic system. Anything that interferes with spinal fluid flow prevents this movement and raises the pressure on the membranes as well as the tissues of the brain or the spinal cord. All of this can result in pain from your head to your tail, as well as emotional and behavioral problems.

Craniosacral therapy is intended to relieve the pressure that interferes with the flow of spinal fluid with gentle pressure to the bones of the skull. For more information, contact the Upledger Institute at 800-233-5880.

CHAPTER 10

Essential Oil Therapy

FOR THOUSANDS OF years, mankind has benefited from the healing properties of plant oils. Incense and aromatic oils have been used for millennia to enhance religious rituals, for embalming, or simply to mask unpleasant odors. It wasn't until the 1920s, though, that essential oil therapy became a formal discipline within health care.

Essential oils are the aromatic substances extracted from various plant parts—these include flowers, roots, bark, leaves, wood resins, and citrus rinds. They can be sprayed into the air and inhaled or absorbed through the skin via massage, in hot baths, or from hot or cold compresses. Some essential oils can be taken internally, but we do not recommend this because a few are toxic when ingested. Essential oils are extracted in concentrated form; but by the time you buy them they have been combined with other carrier oils.

Essential oils improve your mood and promote good health. Some soothe, some relax, some stimulate and invigorate. They

"To His Surprise, the Pain and Redness Subsided Very Quickly"

It happened serendipitously when René-Maurice Gattefosse, a French chemist working in the perfume industry, burned his hand very badly. The only "therapy" immediately available to him was a container of pure lavender oil into which he plunged his scorched hand. To his surprise, the pain and redness subsided very quickly, and Gattefosse claimed that the burn healed within hours without leaving a scar. The chemist attributed this salutary effect to the healing and antiseptic properties of the lavender oil. He experimented with several other oils and decided that they, too, had potential for healing a variety of skin disorders. Other French physicians, notably Dr. Jean Valnet, began to use aromatic oils not only for skin problems but for other medical disorders as well, such as anxiety and insomnia. Valnet, who served as an army surgeon during World War II, treated burns and other wounds with essential oils such as clove, thyme, and chamomile. He also found that certain fragrances alleviated some psychiatric problems.

From *Dr. Rosenfeld's Guide to Alternative Medicine*

work by reacting with hormones and enzymes after they enter the bloodstream. They may affect your pulse, blood pressure, or evoke specific memories. For example, cloves, rosemary, lavender, and mint stimulate the salivary glands; camphor, calamus, and hyssop oils are good for the heart and circulation; other aromatics act on the lymphatic, endocrine, nervous, and urinary systems; oils such as bergamot, lavender, and juniper have antiseptic properties, and when applied to the skin, are said to help a variety of dermatologic disorders.

Calming and comforting oils include sage, sandalwood, patchouli, thyme, jasmine, chamomile, oregano, marjoram, and lavender. Sesquiterpenes, found in the oils of frankincense and sandalwood, help increase the amount of oxygen in the limbic system of the brain, leading to an increase in opioids. Lavender is one of the most popular plants used in essential oil therapy. It is known for its relaxing and calming effects (and is also an excellent remedy for headaches and insomnia). For gentle relaxation, try soaking a tea towel in warm water infused with lavender. You can re-warm the towel in a microwave and bring the lavender scent to your face and hands to experience this aromatic relaxation.

Invigorating herbal oils include mountain savory, peppermint, spearmint, ginger, citrus, mint, and cardamom. Oils that promote clarity of thought are petitgrain, rosemary, cedarwood, basil, spruce, ginger, fir, bergamot, and clove. Oils that are emotionally healing include cypress, eucalyptus, and wild tansy. Oils that increase spiritual awareness and promote emotional harmony and balance are frankincense, galbanum, grapefruit, melissa, myrrh, yarrow, and juniper. To improve sleep, try chamomile, lavender, or marjoram.

Inhalation

Pleasant aromas can lift your mood, help you sleep, and aid in relaxation. When we inhale a particular scent, it is picked up by two small patches of tissue in the nasal cavity. These patches contain more than twenty million nerve endings that can be stimulated by scent. The scent is converted into a nerve message that is immediately transmitted to the limbic system of the brain, which then relays the aroma to the hypothalamus gland, triggering both emotional and physiological responses.

Infusion is a good way to get the most benefit from herbs and flowers. An infusion is just a liquid (water or oil) with an aromatic plant added. By steeping the plant in the liquid, the essence of the plant is extracted. You can do this yourself using small jars with tight-fitting lids (but do not use plastic containers). Place a couple large handfuls of herbs or flowers in a saucepan. Use a neutral-flavored vegetable oil (canola or corn

What Science Says About Essential Oils

Here is what some scientifically valid studies report on the benefits of aromas:

Sleep: In a recent report in the *Lancet,* elderly patients who required substantial doses of sleeping pills slept like babies when a lavender aroma was wafted into their bedrooms at night.

Behavior: Mice made hyper-excitable by large amounts of caffeine were calmed by fragrances of lavender, sandalwood, and other oils sprayed into their cages. On the other hand, they became more irritable when exposed to the aroma of orange terpenes, thymol, and certain other substances.

Stress: At Memorial Sloan-Kettering Hospital in New York, after exposure to the aroma of vanilla, patients reported that they were 63 percent less claustrophobic. The patients' anxiety may have been lessened by the intensity of the pleasant memories evoked by the vanilla aroma. In another study of 122 patients under obvious stress in an intensive care unit, patients felt much better when they were given aromatherapy with oil of lavender than when they simply rested or had a massage.

Isadore Rosenfeld, M.D.[2]

is good) to cover the herbs or flowers. Heat at a low temperature for twenty to thirty minutes, let the oil cool, strain it into a jar, close tightly, and store in a cool, dark place for up to three weeks. To fill a room with the aroma, place the opened jar on a table. You can also pour some oil in your bathwater or rub it on your body after bathing.[1]

Exacting care must be taken when using a diffuser that contains an essential oil, to prevent inhaling it into the lungs. Certain oils must be used with caution as they are known allergenics. Too much of any type of oil might result in an abnormal response. Rosemary appears to have a hyperglycemic (high blood sugar) effect. Eucalyptus citriodora has been found to have a blood sugar lowering effect.

Topical Application

Oils can be applied directly to the skin, typically using one to six drops of oil (though one to three drops is usually adequate). Oil placed on the feet is rapidly absorbed because of large pores. The ears and the wrists will also rapidly absorb the oils. If you are massaging a large area of the body, dilute the oils by about 30 percent with a neutral-smelling vegetable oil.

Don't try and create your own blends of different essential oils. There are commercially available blends that have been formulated by people who understand the chemical nature of each oil and how they blend. The chemical properties can be altered if mixed improperly, and you can get an undesirable reaction. It is better to layer individual oils, applying one oil at a time, rubbing it in, and then applying another oil.

Oils and Water

Essential oils mixed with water can be very pleasing and relaxing. You can fill a water basin with hot water, stir in essential oils, and lay a towel on top of the water to make a compress. The oils will float to the top, so the towel will absorb the oils in the water. After the towel is completely saturated, wring it out and place it over the area of your body needing the compress. Or you can add three to six drops of oil to your bathwater while the tub is filling. Your skin will quickly draw the oil from the top of the water as you soak for about fifteen minutes. Or you can add three to six drops of oil to a half-ounce of bath or shower gel base and add it to your bath water. Here's another option— when showering, you can add three to six drops of oil to a bath or shower gel and apply it to a washcloth.

Raindrop Therapy

Gary Young of Young Essential Oils, an aromatologist and expert on the art and science of aromatherapy, has developed an application technique called raindrop therapy. This involves dropping oils directly onto the spine from about six inches above the body. The oils are worked into the spine with light strokes that stimulate energy impulses and disperse the oil along the nervous system. This is believed to bring the body into balance. A raindrop massage lasts about forty-five minutes, but the oils continue to work in the body for a week or more following the therapy. Oils used in raindrop therapy are Valor (a blend of rosewood, blue tansy, frankincense, and spruce), thyme, oregano, cypress, birch, basil, peppermint, marjoram, and Aroma Siez (a blend of basil, lavender, cypress, and marjoram).

Vita Flex Therapy

Vita Flex Therapy is part of a system developed by Stanley Burroughs using the reflex system of the body to release tension. It combines using essential oils with a form of massage similar to reflexology for the whole body. When applied with rotation hand movements, a healing energy is released along the neuro-electrical pathways. Healing energy is created by the contact between the fingertips and contact points. The resulting energy follows the neuro-pathways of the nervous system to points where there is a break in the electrical circuit. This technique is believed to have originated in Tibet, many thousands of years ago, before acupuncture was discovered. Vita Flex therapists say this is a superior form of reflexology. Although it utilizes the same principles, Vita Flex produces less discomfort than reflexology. In addition, there are about five thousand identified Vita Flex points in the body, compared to only 365 acupuncture points used in reflexology. Combining the electrical energy with the healing properties of essential oils releases healing power, relieving tension, drowsiness, weariness, and discomfort. Oils used in Vita Flex Therapy are Valor and White Angelica (a blend of ylang ylang, rose, angelica, melissa, sandalwood, geranium, spruce, myrrh, hyssop, bergamot, and rosewood).

The following guidelines for use of essential oils come from Isadore Rosenfeld, M.D.:

• Aromatic oils vary in quality, and their production is not regulated. So make sure your source is reliable. Always ask for the purest available brand.
• Do not consume aromatic oils internally. Some can be toxic.
• Store aromatic oils in a cool place. Some oils, such as jasmine and neroli, should be refrigerated. Most retain their potency for two to three years, but citrus oils "die" within a year.

- With the exception of topical lavender oil for burns or insect bites, never use concentrated, undiluted oil. Refer to a good book on aromatherapy for instructions on diluting oil.
- If your skin is sensitive, always apply a very small amount of the diluted oil before you try the whole treatment, to ensure that you're not allergic to it. Five percent of the population reacts adversely to aromatic oils.
- Keep all aromatic oils away from children.
- Always close your eyes when inhaling aromatic oil. The "fumes" can be irritating at close range. Don't apply any oils close to your eyes.
- Do not use mint oils at night, because they can cause insomnia.
- Avoid oils of sweet fennel and rosemary if you have epilepsy. These substances may increase the excitability of the brain and induce seizures.
- If you're pregnant, avoid oils of arnica, basil, clary sage, cypress, juniper, myrrh, sage, and thyme. Some obstetricians believe that these oils can cause the uterus to contract. A woman who is at risk of a miscarriage, or who has abnormal bleeding, should keep away from chamomile and lavender. If your doctor approves it, you may use diluted oils of peppermint, rose, and rosemary after the fourth month of pregnancy.
- People with high blood pressure should avoid oils of rosemary, sage, and thyme.

For more information or to order essential oils, call Young Living at 800-371-3515.

CHAPTER 11

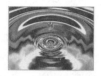

Support People

A SUCCESSFUL RECOVERY involves developing new and more meaningful social networks. That means finding resources and making contacts that will enable you to meet new people who can offer more than just drinking company. As you replace drug use with meaningful, enduring values and activities, you will want to associate with people who share those same values.

They say in AA that to find sobriety you must change playgrounds and playmates. The people you associated with while using are tied to your addiction-based lifestyle. It is not that they are bad; you just have one central thing in common with them—your use of mood-altering substances. If you choose to spend most of your time hanging around old using buddies, their expectations for you to use chemicals can become stressful or even impossible to ignore.

As for "the playgrounds," it has been said that no one frequents a house of ill repute to listen to the piano player. By the same token, you do not go to a bar to have orange juice. In addition, it is not just a question of not associating with your old friends or not frequenting your old hangouts. It is more a question of what new places you are going to and what new friends you are meeting. Your playgrounds will change automatically as you meet new sober people.

Being a social animal is different from being a "party animal." Becoming social is an art; being a party animal is nothing more than getting high or drunk, laughing a lot, acting crazy, and not remembering what you did or said.

Reorienting your lifestyle around values not centered around using is an essential part of recovery. The values that you developed to allow yourself to keep using will not allow you to stay sober. A lifestyle conducive to using is not conducive to sobriety. Friends who encourage drinking or using do not usually encourage abstinence. Places where it is easy to drink or use are not usually places where it is easy not to. New friends, new activities, and new social contacts are part of recovery.

Mutual-Help Groups

A mutual-help group is a valuable source for establishing or re-establishing a meaningful social network. You will find that these people will understand not only your struggles but your need for deeper and more meaningful relationships. They will offer you friendship, support, acceptance, and encouragement. They provide fun, worthwhile activities without alcohol or other drugs. Don't forget how important it is to learn to have fun—especially with individuals who do not focus their good times around mood-altering chemicals.

In recovery you need the support of others, especially the support of people with the same condition. For those who have problems relating to the principles or practices of twelve step groups, there are other support groups available. Most groups encourage a new way of life based on honesty and reaching out to others. They offer a way and a means for making right changes at the right time. They are based on members sharing their experiences and what has worked for them. These groups are places where you can meet people with whom you can feel safe and comfortable in new and healthy ways as you attempt to understand the disorder you have and share with those in the same boat.

Alcoholics Anonymous (AA)

The most well-known support group is Alcoholics Anonymous (AA), founded in the 1930s by people who had tried many other methods of abstaining from alcohol and failed. They found that mutual support gave them a tool that enabled them to do what had previously been unattainable. AA has endured over the years, and these principles apply to other twelve-step programs such as Narcotics Anonymous, Overeaters Anonymous, Cocaine Anonymous, and Gamblers Anonymous.

Alcoholics Anonymous is especially helpful for individuals who prefer a spiritually-based group. The steps of AA are spiritual in nature. In AA you are encouraged to accept the help of a higher power, though that power can be defined as you choose. It can even be the power of the group itself.

Alcoholics Anonymous offers the recovering person many benefits that professional treatment cannot. It offers a readily available environment that is conducive to ongoing recovery and sobriety. AA is available twenty-four hours a day in every major city around the world. You are never farther away from a meeting than the telephone. In large metropolitan areas, meetings are held at all times of the day and night. You can always have the phone number of someone who will help you avoid that one drinking or drug episode.

Alcoholics Anonymous doesn't cost anything—it only

requires your time, energy, and a motivation to stop drinking/using. It is a place to meet others who are interested in having fun and socializing without drugs or alcohol. Many recovering alcoholics/addicts begin the social rebuilding process through friends and acquaintances they find at meetings.

Rational Recovery

Rational Recovery (RR) is an alternative support program utilized primarily by people who are uncomfortable with the spiritual nature of Alcoholics Anonymous. As the name implies, RR is based on the concepts of rational thinking. It was started by Jack Trimpey using the principles of rational-emotive therapy developed by Albert Ellis. In Rational Recovery, you learn to be more aware of your emotions and where they come from. You learn to recognize that emotions are not forced upon you by others or by outside situations. They are your own response to situations, and you can learn to take control of how you respond. Rational Recovery suggests the five-point criteria developed by Maxie Maultsby to evaluate an idea to determine whether it is logical.

1. If I believe this thought to be true, will it help me remain sober, safe, and alive?
2. Is this thought objectively true, and upon what evidence am I forming this opinion?
3. Is this thought producing feelings I want to have?
4. Is this thought helping me reach a chosen goal?
5. Is this thought likely to minimize conflict with others?

Rational Recovery helps you identify irrational ideas and beliefs that perpetuate addictive behavior and then provides the means to change your emotions and behavior.[1]

An AA Sponsor

The principles of AA are simple, though at first can be misunderstood. Therefore, the organization has developed a practice whereby members with a great deal of experience with the program make themselves available to newer members; in other words, they become a sponsor. A sponsor's responsibility is to provide support during recovery, answer questions, discuss the various aspects of the program, assist the new member in identifying meetings that meet their needs, and direct them to appropriate literature and resources that they may need to fully understand the program.

AA sponsors are not therapists or counselors, nor are they responsible for telling other members how to work their programs. All members are responsible for interpreting the principles for themselves and developing their own programs based on those principles. The sponsor is merely a sounding board, a supportive friend, and a knowledgeable resource.

Counseling

If you started drinking or using drugs early in life, you may have skipped some developmental stages of growth. What we mean is that the teens and early twenties are years when emotional and social maturation take place. If drinking and drugging occurred during that time, that developmental process may not have occurred or it may have been retarded.

At whatever point in life you decide to give up drug or alcohol use as a way of coping with life, counseling can aid you in the process of learning to manage your emotions and developing the insights and self-awareness that you may have missed by addictive living.

A counselor can help you resolve pervasive shame that may affect your recovery. Addiction is often accompanied by shame and related emotions for a number of reasons. First, you may feel shame because of a condition that existed before your addiction (such as ADHD) and which increased your vulnerability for using mood altering substances. Second, you may have done things while drinking or using drugs that you would not do sober, and which are very shameful to you now. Third, you may have a history of repeated relapse that you and other people interpret as being weak willed or lacking strength of character. (Actually, the fact that you have kept trying despite what has been perceived as failure shows strong will and strength of character.) And fourth, there is the stigma that accompanies addiction. Our society views addiction as a shameful condition. Even though we live in a culture that encourages drinking, overeating, pill popping, and other excesses, when a person becomes addicted to alcohol, pills, food, or gambling, they are looked upon as morally lacking, self-centered, pleasure-obsessed individuals. Learning to accept yourself as a person of worth despite the burden of shame that you or society has placed upon you can be a positive outcome of counseling. A counselor can help you replace misperceptions you may have about yourself, the world, or your addiction with accurate perceptions that facilitate behavior change.

In recovery you may need to learn or relearn certain life skills. If you want to change behavior, a counselor can help. You have developed many skills that have helped you survive addiction. These same skills can be modified to help you live sober.

David: I am a Reality Therapist. I like Reality Therapy (RT) because it is a very simple approach to helping you change your behavior. It asks you some direct questions that help you evaluate what you are doing and help you make plans to change what you are doing if necessary. The questions are: "What are you doing now?" "Is that working for you?" "If not, what are you going to do instead?" The idea is to figure out what is not working in your life and not just eliminate it but replace it with a better chosen behavior. With RT you take small, manageable steps that lead you where you want to go.

Coaching

Coaching is not counseling. The term *coaching,* taken from sports, refers to an alliance that empowers success. Coaching is now being used to empower professional success, educational success, and personal success. It is being used extensively by people with attention deficit disorder (ADHD coaching). We recommend ADHD coaching for people recovering from addiction. In the first place, many who have had problems with addiction also have ADHD, treated or untreated. Second, many of the symptoms of ADHD are experienced by people in sobriety. Third and most important, many skills that people with ADHD need to develop are lacking in those suffering with addictions. So let's talk about the benefits of coaching.

The purpose of any coaching is to *enhance performance.* The purpose of ADHD coaching is to enable you to enhance performance by helping you (1) set goals, (2) devise a plan for reaching your goals, (3) set priorities, (4) make decisions, and (5) keep on track. The coach offers guidance and support while giving responsibility to you. The first phase in the coaching process is setting the agenda—identifying your long-term goals. And remember—this is your agenda, not the coach's agenda. The second phase is making short-term goals that will meet day-to-day needs and lead to the achievement of your long-term goals. During the second phase it is important to review regularly to determine if the long-term goals are still applicable.

The value of coaching for you will be having someone available to guide you when you find it difficult to sort things out and prioritize tasks. Someone trained to do so can help you keep on track by continually holding up your goals and identifying whether what you are doing will achieve your goals. The coach can help you keep moving when you feel paralyzed by the obstacles you encounter as you face the problems created by your addiction. The coach can also help you identify what supports need to be put in place in order to increase your chances for success, determine what you want or need to accomplish between coaching sessions, and decide what tasks will help you accomplish those things. When you and the coach determine what skills are lacking that prevent you from achieving your goals you will make plans for developing those skills or change your goals according to the skills you already have. The greatest value of having a coach is having someone to provide regular reminders of where you want to go and what you need to do to get there.

Coaching differs from counseling in that the power lies not in the coach or the client, but in the coaching alliance. The client is a full partner in the alliance. The coach's goal is always to facilitate the client's agenda. By asking powerful and direct questions, reminding you of your agenda, and keeping you focused, the coach allows you to plan your own course and take the steps to keep you on it. The alliance provides a safe environment for you to practice developing life skills. The phone number for the American Coaching Association is 610-825-8572.

CHAPTER 12

Stress-Reducing Activities

STRESS AFFECTS YOUR body and your mind. It affects your thinking, feelings, ability to remember, sleep patterns, daily functioning, and physical and mental health. When a sudden alert is sounded in the body, the center part of the brain (the hypothalamus) sends a message to the adrenal gland to release cortisol. Cortisol increases the heart rate, increases the blood pressure, and releases stored glucose from the liver and muscle cells into the bloodstream for quick energy.

Stress has almost become a bad word in our modern society. The truth is, though, that some stress in life is necessary. It keeps you functioning. Without some stress you would not take care of yourself, go to work, or do anything for your family. But too much stress is harmful. Each of us has a level of stress at which we function most effectively. Your best stress level is high enough to keep you productive, yet low enough not to hurt you or the people around you. Finding the level of stress that is useful without being destructive is important in your recovery from addiction. You can relapse because of too little stress (no constructive concern about your addiction) or because of too much stress (which produces excessive worry and anxiety).

One of the most agonizing abstinence symptoms is stress sensitivity. Most recovering people have a low stress tolerance and overreact to stress. As we have discussed before, this can sabotage even the best efforts at sobriety. We have talked about foods and supplements and environmental changes to reduce stress levels. There are also actions you can take to reduce stress and increase serenity and peace of mind. The relaxation response (the decrease of blood pressure and pulse rate and the improved utilization of oxygen) occurs because of what you do and think. You can learn to relax.

Deep Relaxation

You're probably aware that your muscles cannot relax and tense at the same time. You can learn to relax your muscles when you choose, thereby reducing tension. You can also learn to form images in your mind that help you relax. And you can learn to talk to yourself in a way that reduces tension and increases your feelings of comfort and well-being.

Deep relaxation allows the body and mind to reduce stress and produce a sense of well-being. What occurs when you relax is the opposite of what is called the "fight-or-flight" reaction. Upon relaxing, your muscles become heavy, your body temperature rises, and your breathing and heart rate slow down.

To experience deep relaxation, create a quiet place for yourself. Separate yourself from the world in your quiet place. Lie on your back or sit in a comfortable chair with your feet on the floor. Close your eyes, release distracting thoughts, try to put background noises and sounds out of your thoughts. Breathe deeply and relax your body. You do not make your body relax, you allow it to relax. You focus on one thing and allow distractions to drift from your awareness.

With some relaxation methods, the focus is on the physical states you are trying to change (your muscles, body temperature, breathing, or heartbeat). With other methods, you do not concentrate on your physical state, but on a color, a sound, a word or mantra, or a mental image.

If you choose to focus on physical states, begin with your muscles. Allow them to become heavy. Then concentrate on raising your temperature. You can do this by sensing a spot of heat in your forehead or chest and allowing it to flow throughout your body. Then think about your breathing. Let it become slower and slower; breathe from your abdomen rather than your chest. Then feel your heartbeat and concentrate on slowing it down.

If you choose to relax by concentrating on something other than your physical state, you can think of a color. Concentrate on that color, fill your mind with that color, become a part of that color. Or feel yourself in motion, floating, tumbling, and rolling. Or repeat a pleasant word over and over to yourself. Or imagine yourself in a soothing place, such as by a quiet lake, in a green meadow, or at a beach. These are relaxation exercises you can do by yourself without the aid of a book or a tape.

There are numerous books and tapes available to guide you through the relaxation process. Or you can record a tape yourself and play it when you want to relax. Deep relaxation reduces your stress and helps you feel better. Relaxation exercises can help you manage abstinence symptoms and heal your addicted brain.

Breathing

Deep breathing aids in relaxation. In his newsletter, Self-Healing, Dr. Andrew Weil has noted that deep breathing has been shown to lower blood pressure, decrease or stop heart arrhythmias, improve digestion, increase blood circulation, decrease anxiety, and improve the quality of sleep. To distinguish deep breathing from shallow breathing, pay attention to your chest and your abdomen. Chest breathing is usually shallow breathing; abdominal breathing is usually deep breathing.

Dr. Weil describes a yoga-style method of breathing like this: Start by sitting with your back straight or lying in a comfortable position. Place the tip of your tongue to the ridge in back of your upper front teeth and keep it there during the entire exercise. Exhale through the mouth with a whoosh sound. Close your mouth and inhale through your nose to the count of four. Hold your breath for seven counts and then exhale, with the whoosh sound, to the count of eight. Do this for four cycles.

There is a connection between breathing and your emotional state. Fear, anger, and frustration restrict breathing. Restricted breathing increases negative emotional states. Your sense of well-being can be enhanced by your breathing. When you calm your breath you calm your mind. Calming your breathing throughout the day brings a sense of peacefulness. The constitution of the blood is altered through oxygen exchange which, in turn, leads to more relaxed breathing. Here is another deep breathing exercise you can try:

1. While sitting or lying down, place your hands on your stomach and chest.
2. Sigh (audibly) several times.
3. Slowly and fully inhale through the mouth, filling the lungs

comfortably from the bottom to the top. Imagine you are bringing energy into your body.

4. Without hesitation, allow the air to be exhaled through the nose, emptying the lungs from the top to the bottom in a comfortable manner. Visualize yourself releasing your tensions as you breathe out.

5. Repeat this procedure for ten to fifteen minutes, until you are totally and pleasantly absorbed with the breathing process and alert but not focusing on any other thoughts or processes. There will be a feeling of peace and serenity just in controlling your breathing process.

Yoga

Developed over centuries, yoga is used to reduce stress, improve flexibility, and provide mental clarity. Yoga is a technique with three major components: posture, breathing, and meditation. The first objective of yoga is to maintain one of a variety of yoga poses for a specified period of time. The ultimate goal is to gain the self control needed for proper breathing and for effective meditation. The breathing exercises consist of a routine in which the lungs are filled with air which is held and then released.

The goal of the meditation component is to detach from your environment and to experience "peace, enlightenment, and tranquility."

Here is a scaled-down version of yoga that you can follow easily and effectively, as described in the University of Texas–Houston Lifetime Health Letter[1]:

• *For exercise:* Sit forward in a chair, your feet flat on the floor. Put your right hand on your left knee. With your left hand, hold the back of the chair. Look straight ahead, inhale, and then as you slowly exhale, turn to your left. Pull with both hands to rotate your spine as much as possible without strain. Hold the rotated position for a few seconds, continuing to breathe easily. Return to the forward position. Then put your left hand on your right knee, and repeat the steps, twisting to the right.

- *For breathing:* Sit straight with both hands flat against your stomach, just below the navel. Relax your stomach and allow it to push out as you inhale. Then, as you exhale, tighten your stomach and flatten your back. Concentrate on the sound your breath makes in the back of your throat. Breathe smoothly and steadily through your nose; don't hold your breath at any time. Repeat this procedure several times.
- *For meditation:* Sit quietly and comfortably in a chair or on the floor. Close your eyes and take a few full, deep breaths. Concentrate on the sound you make when you breathe in and out. Relax your breath, and at the same time, consciously relax your facial muscles. Progressively relax the rest of your body, beginning with the shoulders and arms, working your way down to your feet. Become limp without slouching. Try to be completely silent, inside and out. Imagine a pleasant scene to help yourself achieve total relaxation. After a few minutes, begin to breathe more deeply; then stretch your arms and imagine your energy being totally renewed.

Several scientific reports suggest that yoga can reduce blood pressure and heart rate and improve circulation. It can help you relax and ease chronic pain. It can improve your memory and help you concentrate. Some of these benefits may be due to a release of opioids.

Contact the International Association of Yoga Therapists (415-383-4587) for the name of a yoga practioner in your neck of the woods.

Sleep

Sleep is an important ingredient of good health. Because of an addictive lifestyle, you may have developed poor sleep habits. In addition, you may experience abstinence-related sleep problems. This may be especially true if you have used alcohol excessively in the past. Although alcohol is sedating, it disrupts normal sleep patterns and deprives you of REM sleep (dream sleep). When you are no longer drinking, there is a rebound effect in which your body tries to catch up on lost REM sleep and, for a period of time, you may experience an excessive amount of disturbing dreams.

To enhance the quality of recovery, you may need to enhance the quality and quantity of sleep. Some general considerations are:

- Be sure the temperature of the room is comfortable for you.
- Maintain regular sleeping times by going to sleep and waking at the same times each day.
- Avoid exercising close to bedtime. Exercise is a stimulant and can disturb your sleep.
- Avoid stimulant substances such as caffeine (or tyrosine) near bedtime.
- Take a warm bath.
- Listen to music.
- Do relaxation exercises.
- Eat a high-tryptophan bedtime snack.
- Choose your mattress and pillows carefully. Make sure your weight is evenly distributed. Make sure your pillow provides enough support for your neck.

Physical Exercise

David and I have a friend who used to say, "I have a theory that exercise causes cancer. The only thing I exercise is caution. I only enjoy long walks when they are taken by people who nag me to exercise." She was kidding, of course, but behind the humor she was saying something many people would like to say, "We would like a good excuse not to exercise and any good theory will do." The interesting thing we want you to know is that our friend has discovered that she is diabetic and, following her doctor's direction, began walking every day. She had to start gradually and work up. She now walks two miles every day and, in addition to helping her control her diabetes, her walk has become a high point of her day. She will readily tell you how beneficial exercise is and how much it has helped her not just physically but mentally.

Our purpose here is not to convince you that you should endure the physical pain of exercise to reap the gain. It is to encourage you to establish an exercise program in order to relieve the pain you may already be experiencing. The whole purpose of this book is to provide options for increasing pleasure, not pain, in sobriety. We are not going to discuss the benefits of exercise on your heart or lungs or for weight loss. You probably already know how important exercise is for your general health. Our purpose is to remind you of the benefits in reducing your stress by changing your brain chemistry. Certainly, exercise is important to your physical health. What we want to offer you is the pleasure reward that you can get from physical movement.

The truth is that physical activity can be fun, stimulating, and relaxing. A good exercise plan can add pleasure instead of pain to life. The trick is finding a physical activity that is right for you, something you enjoy doing. No one sticks to an exercise program that is not enjoyable.

Move Your Body: It's Good for You

"To be alive is to be moving. The unmoving water becomes the stagnant pool. The moving body freely channels the energy of life. Moving encourages movement. The more you move, the better you move. Energy creates energy—in a continuous, circling process—in a constant dance. Exercise makes us feel good—not just physically, but emotionally and spiritually. As if the physical advantages of exercise were not enough, its connection to the ways we think and feel about ourselves is remarkable. The moving body is the body releasing stress, letting go of pent-up emotions and unblocking channels for energy."

from *The Wellness Workbook*[2]

The more we move, the better we feel, the more motivated we are to move, and the more energy we have. We feel enlivened when we move. Movement allows us to feel our muscles work, our heart beat, and the blood flow through our bodies, creating energy and a feeling of well-being.

Many recovering people have found exercise to be extremely helpful in freeing them from the limitations of abstinence symptoms. We know many recovering addicts who stop in the middle of their day's activities to exercise when they are feeling anxious or having difficulty concentrating or remembering. After exercising they feel much better and are more productive (and easier to get along with). Researchers at the University of North Carolina-Greensboro found that aerobic exercise reduces depression and anxiety levels in alcoholics.

Research indicates that exercise actually neutralizes brain chemicals that otherwise would increase craving for mood-altering substances. According to the National Center for Health Statistics, frequent exercisers have higher levels of endorphins and demonstrate more positive moods and less anxiety than those who exercise too little or not at all.

David: Different forms of exercise have different payoffs for me. I have chosen these forms of exercise as strengthening contributions to my sobriety. Hiking or taking a long vigorous walk gives me "special time" to be completely alone with myself and my God, to meditate and to pray.

I find that movement of my body up hills and down inclines in the heart of nature allows me to think more clearly, often resolving issues or making short-range plans. I find that a walk enables me to break out of the dull stupor that daily routine can bring. Because I automatically feel good while walking, my awareness of my surroundings is also sharpened as if a newly discovered sense is emerging. I then begin to think in a more positive way about myself and my life. I feel more in control of my life. By the end of the walk I am ready to meet new challenges with a new sense of inner strength.

Tennis or some "involvement sport" relaxes me in another way. It provides strenuous exercise with almost every muscle being used, and with complete awareness of my physical self. It feels good to reach out and slam the ball, providing a surge of power and energy and anger release.

Fellowship with my partner is also healthy and relaxing for me. Even though we are competing, it is all in fun. There is laughing, yelling, and just plain "letting go."

Swimming is my "special" activity. I know of no other recreation that allows me more feelings of surrender. When I let go and become part of the water, I seem to flow through it with my worries and tension dissolving. Exercise is a vital part of my sobriety program and improves the quality of my life.

Aerobic Exercise

Regular exercise in which we use the whole body and keep moving at a steady pace—dancing, jogging, walking, swimming, bicycling—is aerobic and not only relieves stress and gives us a lift, but burns fat. Aerobic exercise increases oxygen intake. Increasing oxygen increases endorphins. While we do not recommend that you limit yourself to aerobic exercise, we strongly recommend that you participate in some aerobic activity every day. It is a good idea to have a variety of activities from which to choose so that an exercise plan is not dependent on partners or on the weather.

Walking is an excellent form of aerobic exercise that is available to anybody. Walking can reduce tension and anxiety immediately. It is one of the most efficient forms of exercise and can be done safely throughout your life. It is also inexpensive and does not require special equipment other than good shoes. It offers the extra benefit of giving you time to reflect and organize your thoughts.

Walking can easily be incorporated into your daily activity. Maybe you can walk to work or to the bank, post office, or to visit a friend. Try taking the stairs instead of an elevator. Walk around the airport while waiting for your plane.

Stretching

Stretching exercises for warming up and cooling down will make your body more flexible. We recommend that you use stretching exercises throughout your day to relax muscles, reduce stiffness, and ease tension.

It is especially helpful to relax the muscles of your neck and shoulders throughout the day. Many people store a lot of tension in this area. Raise both of your shoulders at the same time and slowly rotate them in a circle, backward and then for-

Stress-Relief Tip

For a short tension reliever and also to improve circulation to the extremities, including the head, try placing the palms of your hands on your eyes for a few minutes. Follow this by placing your hands on the back of your head and twisting your body right and left while still seated. While your hands are still placed on the back of your head, touch each elbow to the knee on the same side and then back into the resting position.

Now, place one hand up and over behind your head, touching your back, and place the other hand on the opposite elbow and stretch. Alternately, bend the knees to the chest, one at a time, while sitting on a chair. Next, stretch by placing your feet and hands as far back on each side of the chair as you are able. Complete this exercise with a moment of relaxation by again placing your palms on your eyes and breathing deeply.

Diana W. Guthrie[3]

ward. Then roll your head around several times in a full circle as you keep your back straight.

Another place that many people store tension is in the lower back. To strengthen and relax those muscles, lie on your back with knees bent and feet flat on the floor. Tighten your abdominal muscles, grip your buttocks together, and flatten your lower back against the floor. Repeat this several times. Then bring one leg toward your chest. Pull the leg to your chest with your hands. Slowly curl your head toward your bent knee and hold for a count of five. Repeat the exercise with the other leg. Then do the exercise with both legs simultaneously. If you do these exercises for a few minutes every day, you will prevent or reduce much strain in your lower back.

Fun, Laughter and Humor

Fun is a necessary part of life and of recovery, and it is often neglected. It is not only a part of recovery; it is an essential ingredient of life. Learning to enjoy life naturally will take time and practice because in the past fun has occurred unnaturally through mind-altering chemicals. So it will take some time to convince yourself that you do have the ability to have fun, to enjoy and celebrate without altering your mood artificially. You have the ability to create pleasure in natural ways. Fun and laughter relate directly to the production of opioids. Fun is first and foremost a change of attitude, reaction, and perception about yourself as you slow down and experience life in the present.

Play is usually perceived as something separate and apart from life. Fun is seen as the icing of life; as long as you get your work done you can then, and only then, have fun. Life should be fun and fun a priority, not something we do when and/or if we have time. We can become so serious about eating right and getting regular exercise that we never allow ourselves to have fun. Life without fun is like a long dental appointment.

From time to time take breaks in your schedule that add color, spontaneity, and some zaniness to life. Put on your favorite music, sing, dance around the room, and let the child in you out. Have a water fight. Make yourself up like a clown. Get silly with the one you love. See what you can think of that is a little crazy and a lot of fun. Find people that you can have fun with, people that can let go and try new things.

Do you ever watch children having fun? They do not make a distinction between work and play. Play is their work. They play when they walk, talk, or when they are putting together puzzles. They are constantly using their developing senses to explore this new world and, for the most part are happy with their exploration. Don't let society's messages to "act your

Children and Laughter: The Best Medicine

Look for things all around you to laugh about. We keep a notebook of funny things children in our family have said. These are some favorites:

- "My teeth are shivering."
- "God made me an eating person."
- "You plug it in and I'll plug it out."
- "Why are you sleeping with your breakfast?" (To someone eating in bed.)
- "I need a couple of water."
- "A ghost is hollow on the inside and doesn't have any shell on the outside."
- "Don't call Mom the old lady. She's no lady."
- "Sometimes I snore when I laugh."
- "Trix are for folks, too. You can have some; you're a folk."

age" or "grow up" or "stop being foolish" deprive you of the richness of life that play offers.

You may be so programmed to believe that playing is wasting time that you need permission to play. Well, we give you permission. You must play for your health, your well-being, and your recovery. You will find that you are able to accomplish more if you take time for play than if you neglect it. We can learn about play from children. Observe how they give themselves to each moment, allowing them to enjoy and experience whatever they are doing.

Fun is its own reward. Fun feels good, and it enables us to feel good about ourselves.

True enjoyment is characterized by laughter. Laughter

At Play
by David

Come, child, blend with me.
The time is now, as only time can be.
Come, child, let me share your world where pain is a stranger,
and glances laced with sweet innocence,
dance on a world made just for you.

Come, child, let me into your eyes.
Share your world where time has no back or front,
just a middle where all is now
as you contemplate some beauty of nature
cast in this plant or that bug.
Come, child, I will honor this time
where we may touch this now together,
as I learn of your wisdom
that I passed so blindly by on the path to "adult."

Come, child, allow me into your joyful laughter—
that clean innocent music where love and joy were born.
Come, child, remind me through your dancing eyes
of when I, too, was eternal and praised the world
through uncluttered observations, never mindful or
caring of expectations the world was casting my way,
dulling my senses through its call to sameness,
where wrong is to be different, where it's wrong to be me.

Come, child, teach me your ways once again
and allow me into your space to rest,
to find forgotten fragments of my self,
to reacquaint myself with the magic moment,
to be all that I can be—here and now.

The Clown Chakra

The Clown Scientists have found that all our problems can be placed under one heading: "Seriousness." Seriousness is the leading cause of everything from cancer to reincarnation.

Scientists from the Clown Academy have already discovered a new source of healing. It is a psychic energy point located between the heart chakra and the throat chakra. It is called the Clown Chakra.

If people are feeling miserable, if they have financial problems, if their relationship situation is the pits, if they are in ill health, if they have a need to sue people, if they find fault with their brother, then obviously, their Clown Chakra is closed.

When this happens, the scientists have observed under a high-powered microscope that the cells of every organ display a sad face, and, when the Clown Chakra is open and functioning normally, the cells display a happy face.

The scientists realized that, if a person is ill, it is because his mind has projected guilt onto the cells of his body and has forced out the love that is normally found within each cell of the body. The cells are therefore saying, "I Lack Love," or "ILL" for short.

The scientists also discovered that all disease is due to the fact that the cells are out of ease, or dis-eased.

When the Clown Chakra is opened and working (or rather, playing) properly, the psychic mechanism sucks up misery, pain, anger, resentment, grievances, unhappiness, etc., and converts the energy into tiny red heart-shaped balloons. The red heart-shaped balloons contain Love and Joy.

These balloons are directed to the dis-eased cell or situation, and a happy face appears instantly. When the light enters the darkness, the darkness is gone. Sometimes these red heart-shaped balloons are called endorphins, due to the fact that, when anyone experiences them, the feeling of separation ends. They experience being back home with All That Is and hence are no longer an orphan. This is the well-known end-orphan (endorphin) effect.

So, if you think someone is attacking you, Clown Scientists recommend that you visualize sending that person red heart-shaped balloons filled with love and joy. Remember to keep your Clown Chakra open and remember to laugh.

releases "feel-good" brain chemicals and lightens our hearts. After we laugh we feel better, we think better, and we function better. You must laugh for your health, your well-being, and your recovery.

Humor helps us adapt to change. Recovery requires a lot of change. Why not make it easier on yourself by seeing the humor and learning to laugh at yourself? Laughing at yourself allows you to give yourself permission to be imperfect. And when you can find humor in your own imperfections, it is easier to accept imperfections in others.

Research shows that laughter increases creativity and the ability to mentally organize information. Studies also show that humor, laughter, or mild elation enables people to remember, make decisions, and figure things out better. It seems this "feel good" stuff is just what a person with abstinence symptoms needs. Lighten up. Laugh a lot. It can only do you good.

Laughter is life's shock absorber. It allows you to take yourself lightly while taking other things seriously. Laughter is internal jogging, and you don't have to get dressed to do it.

Consider this old Japanese proverb, "Time spent laughing is

time spent with the gods." Garrison Keillor says it this way: "Humor is not a trick. Humor is a presence in the world . . . like grace . . . and shines on everybody."

Pets

It is well-documented that pets can improve our health. Studies have shown that our enjoyment of our pets raises our spirits, lowers our blood pressure and cholesterol, and overall just makes life more enjoyable. Their unique, unconditional relationship with us helps us feel appreciated and important.

Did someone mention pets?

Did you ask about Sammy? Well, since you ask, we just happen to have pictures. He is our seven-pound Papillion who we named Samson because he hasn't the faintest idea he isn't a Great Dane. He keeps us laughing with his antics: trying to cram a ball and a bone in his mouth at the same time, trying to jump up on a bed with a toy bigger than he is, or carrying around an empty plastic bottle big enough for him to climb into. He just doesn't know limits. What Sam lacks in weight he makes up for in determination and speed. Just when you think he's in another room, there he is, right on your heels. Like the speed of light. What Sammy is really big on, though, is heart. It's hard to believe so much love and affection can reside in so small a creature. He always wants to be where we are. They say if you like to go to the bathroom alone, don't get a Papillion. Sammy will sit at the door and wait for you to come out. When anyone comes to the house, he always gets extremely excited. We haven't told him that not everyone who comes to the door comes to see him. He gets so excited he gets the "zoomies," zipping around and around the house like he is propelled by a motor. Sammy's special gift is touching. He not only wants to be in the same room with us at all times, he wants to be as close as he can get. He must sleep with us, usually snuggled up against a leg or a butt, kind of like a furry Fixodent. As soon as we stir in the morning, he smothers us with hugs and kisses. He hugs by putting his front paws on our chests and snuggling his face into our necks. Of course, you know what his kisses are, and he always overdoes it, not just with us, but with anyone who can't escape. We are thinking of putting up a sign that says, "Beware, our dog can't hold his licker." Since he has come into our lives, sleep has been more restful, laughter more frequent, and every day brighter. Some people say we are a little overzealous and spoil him a bit. One friend says in his next life he wants to come back as Sammy. But most people who meet him admit that Sammy lights up the place.

Softening the Environment

Overload, high distractibility, hyper-vigilance, and stimulus augmentation all mean principally the same thing. When a person's filtering system does not work well, perception is altered. But you can learn to soften your environment and separate yourself periodically from unpleasant noises and sensations.

David: I may leave home without my American Express card. But I will never leave home without my earplugs! One of the best gifts of my life was a pair of earplugs given to me by a friend that works for General Motors. They have ridges on them that fit comfortably and snugly into the ear and, best of all, they work great. I can still hear with them in, but they soften the noise quite a bit so at least my nervous system doesn't spasm when that "no muffler" car roars by.

In addition to earplugs, a "white-noise" machine might be helpful. These wonderful little gadgets emit a soft, masking sound like a waterfall, an ocean, or similar sound that covers up those clanging, banging noises. A fan or a computer may work because they both emit white noise of their own. Some people leave on the fan to their central air or heat to give them constant white noise. Many of us are truly fans of fans.

There are things that can be done, too, where you live or spend time to quiet the environment. Double-paned glass doors or windows and carpeting on the floor—or even carpeting on the wall—can deaden sound and allow some protection from unwanted sound intrusions. Learn to lower the noise levels in your environment. Tone down the music and turn off the television once in a while. The environment can also be softened with music, overstuffed furniture, simple, "pleasant-to-the-eye" décor, and harmonious colors.

Anne: I used to watch television to help me to shut off my brain. But when I watched the news or a TV program, it seemed to disquiet my mind, and I would go to sleep more agitated. When I moved to Hawaii, I didn't take my TV with me. What I've learned is that TV did not shut off my brain—it gave me more things to think about.

My apartment now is very quiet. Not having constant TV noise makes a big difference. I feel more calm and relaxed without TV in my life. It has made all the difference in the world. It's as if the quietness has helped me to find an "off button." I'm really at peace here. I feel centered, and I like that.

You can learn to separate yourself periodically from the crowded stimuli you live with. Try putting a "Do Not Disturb" sign on the door. Or make time for quiet activities like browsing the library or museum. Or seek the quiet places in the great outdoors. In these ways you can temporarily eliminate noisy, chaotic activities.

Gale: Something that has often helped me is to go to a hot tub or a swimming pool where I float on my back. With my ears just under the water, I hear a roaring sound. The act of floating this way and the white noise that the water creates in my head relaxes and calms me and slows down my thought processes.

But there are good sounds going on in the world, right along with the obnoxious ones. Most of the time, sounds of children playing and laughing can be pleasant. These playful sounds of life can be some of the greatest sounds of all, the sounds of living.

The perception of touch is also affected by stimulus augmentation. Letting people know to what extent you are comfortable being touched is important. It is also important to be comfortable physically with the right shoes and clothing.

Robin: Something that has helped me a lot with my stimulus augmentation is wearing comfortable clothing. When I have on tight or poor-fitting clothes, my stress levels go way up. It's not something most people think of as pertinent when we talk about changing our environment. But it can make a dramatic difference.

Touch

Touching is not just pleasurable, it is a human need. As we have tended to become isolated as a society—distanced as families and neighbors, whether because of the increased use of technology, the impersonal workplace, or our fear of crime and abuse—physical contact has suffered. The skin needs nurturing.

Skin is the body's largest organ and often the most neglected. Be good to your skin by wearing soft clothing made of natural fabrics that breathe. Protect it from sun damage. Use moisturizers to protect it from dryness. Touching is a great source of pleasure. Blood pressure can be lowered by petting a furry animal (especially one like Sammy). A hug can be very therapeutic. "Healing touch" is not just a phrase, it is an experience.

Water

There is a natural healing power to water. We use it for hydration, cleansing, nutrition, relaxation, and recreation. It stimulates, warms, cools, soothes, and fulfills the need for touch.

Showering does more than cleanse. Use it to experience the healing power of water. Try standing under a shower and enjoying the feel of the water on your skin. To awaken your senses and increase circulation, alternate hot and cold water. Try a shower massager, or shower at night with only a night light and imagine that you are standing in a waterfall.

Like a shower, a bath can also be used for more than cleansing. In the bath, water can touch you all over, can embrace you. It can soothe and relax you through its buoyancy, warmth, and gentleness. A hot tub provides much the same luxurious pleasure. In addition, its whirlpool jets can relieve an aching, sore body as well as soothe and relax muscles.

Swimming is one of few activities by which we can get complete exercise and a sensuous experience at the same time. Lap swimming can be meditative as well. If you wear goggles and earplugs, the sound of water gurgling as you swim contributes to the relaxation. Because the water supports every part of the body, this form of exercise can seem effortless. The water supports as it caresses.

It is not necessary to know how to swim to enjoy a dip in a pool. You can do water exercise or just splash and have fun. The weightless feeling is very pleasurable when you can let go and just be. Enjoy the buoyancy of the water by submerging yourself and floating to the top.

Music

Some sounds soothe, and some invigorate. The sounds of music, waterfalls, rustling leaves, ocean waves, or birds singing are usually pleasing and enjoyable. Other sounds are pleasing to some people and not to other people. Be selective and choose sounds that help you feel more comfortable. Careful choice of music or sound can enhance the pleasure of daily life. It can brighten spirits or calm them down, depending on the type of music played.

Music is powerful. Music that is paced at fifty beats per minute is calming and relaxing. It can also provide a quiet background for study. Music energizes the body through vibration. Singing or humming is stress relieving. Music sets the stage for the body to be in balance and thereby supports the healing process.

David: A memorable magic moment occurred for me as I was going through a car wash. A Kenny G CD was on, and as I glided through the suds, I was cleansed by the sounds of the music; just rub-a-dub-dubbing along through the car wash, that sax and I were one. All around the car, music angels were flitting on swooshing wings delivering their rhythmic embrace, fusing me and settling an always fragile equilibrium with soothing resonance and artful elegance. I felt cleaner than the car, my sparkle enhanced by music's medicine.

Music, art, and nature can be especially enjoyable for people with stimulus augmentation. Individuals with the ability to see and hear so much at one time often have an appreciation of details that simply pass others by. When listening to music they hear and experience every instrument. When looking at a painting they are aware of nuances of color not perceived by those less aware. When walking by the ocean they are aware of the sand beneath their feet, the color of the sky, the sound of the seagull, and the grace of the pelican. They notice the size and shape of the shells, the roar of the sea, the regularity of the waves, and the great expanse of the water. And so they have the capacity to experience ecstasy and awe in a way that is unknown to those who can experience only one thing at a time.

CHAPTER 13

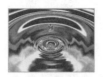

Stress-Reducing Attitudes

WHILE SEARCHING FOR ways to change your physiology and biochemistry to increase your comfort in sobriety, don't forget that how you feel is also determined by your thoughts, feelings, perceptions, perspectives, and beliefs. You are not a victim of your physiology. You are not powerless over your thoughts, feelings, and attitudes. You can choose the way you look at yourself, other people, and the world. In doing so, you also can better your ability to handle stress and the challenges of recovery.

Anxiety Can Be an Opportunity

Anxiety is not necessarily bad. It can call your attention to a need for change, or it can make you mindful of something you've been unaware of. A crisis can be an opportunity.

The question is: are you going to listen to what the anxiety is telling you or run from it? For many of us, anxiety triggers a desire to consume a substance that relieves the anxiety by releasing endorphins that help us relax. When this has been our way of reducing anxiety and we choose not to use that method anymore, we need other ways to decrease anxiety. If we don't find them, our level of anxiety continues to escalate.

You may believe that discomfort is proof that you are doing something wrong. Discomfort does not always mean that there is a problem. It may mean that something wonderful is about to happen. But to get to the other side of anxiety it is necessary to experience it and not try to make it go away. If you face it, it can help you discover what you believe about your situation, yourself, and your life. Pain can motivate you to move toward your dreams. But if your goal is to make it go away, you can usually find a way to do that—but only temporarily. If you can handle the discomfort without looking for pain control, then you may find yourself looking at a new opportunity.

Don't let anxiety get you off the track from where you want to go, whether your goal is staying sober or changing your career. Don't let fear block your dreams. The faith and courage you need to follow your dreams comes from the inner wisdom that knows what you need to do. When you listen to the voice that encourages you to go ahead, one step at a time, the anxiety lessens, and you can walk into opportunities you thought would always remain just dreams. Change demands risk, but change is an exciting part of life. Taking the risk to try something new keeps life exciting and full of surprises.

It May Be in Your Perception

Sometimes anxiety is due to what we perceive is going on, rather than what is actually going on. We interpret events according to our perceptions. If we expect to be rejected, we may perceive that we have been rejected, when in fact we haven't been. If we believe ourselves incapable of doing a good job, we may think we are doing a poor job, when in fact we are doing well.

But anxiety does not always mean that something is wrong with your thinking; sometimes it means something is wrong with someone else's thinking. You can experience anxiety because others do not recognize or support your worth. In such situations, you might choose to avoid a crisis by accepting the other person's belief, but you experience anxiety when you settle for less than you deserve or are capable of.

There is a difference between feeling bad and being bad; the difference between fact and feelings. It is important to identify what your feelings are, respect them, and learn to express them in appropriate ways; but it is also important to recognize that these feelings may be based on inaccuracies. Sometimes, instead of changing our situation, we need to change our perception of it. In order to do that, it is necessary to tolerate discomfort long enough to figure out what the facts really are and what action is appropriate.

Learning to look at a situation differently can increase serenity even when there is nothing you can do to change it. Step back and refocus. Evaluate whether something is worth fighting for. Not every argument is worth trying to win. Set yourself free from the anxiety of unrealistic expectations.

Believe You Can Change

When we are unaware of effective ways to bring about change, we often apply the same would-be cures over and over again more intensely, more diligently. The more ineffective our actions, the harder we try, despite growing despair. If you are trying to pound a nail with a marshmallow, it doesn't help to hit harder. As you come to believe that nothing can be solved, you lose hope of anything getting better. A common statement that shuts out the possibility of change is "That's just the way I am." This is a way of saying, "Don't expect anything different from me. I will always be like I am."

Believing you can achieve something empowers you. This is not just the power of positive thinking. If you believe something is possible, you will invest more energy in making it happen than if you really don't believe it can happen. You have more energy to invest. Hope is energizing. It re-inspires confidence; it fires imagination and creativity. You do have choices, even when you don't know what they are. Feeling powerless is not the same as being powerless.

There are some payoffs in being powerless to change. Some of us get nurturing from being helpless; most of us do to some extent. Painful situations allow us to nurture ourselves in certain ways because we "deserve it." After all, look at what we have suffered. We may believe we would have to give up nurturing ourselves if it was no longer a reward for our suffering.

Are people with an addiction victims? Well, in a sense, yes: victims of physiology. You didn't choose your body. If you were born that way, it certainly isn't your fault, and even those things you've done to contribute to the problem you did in the sincere attempt to make things better. People with addictions are also victims of public opinion and prejudice, but because this condition is not your fault does not mean you are not responsible for the choices you make as a result. It may be that heredity, your environment, and society have contributed to your situation. But regardless of the contributing factors, you are the one that has to do something about it.

You can change. People change all the time. Change is a part of life. Believing you can do something not only gives you hope, it increases your chances for success. If you go to the gym and work out, you are not creating new muscles; you are just making the ones you already have stronger. The same is true for the abilities you need to change. You already have them. You just need to strengthen them. The most essential ingredient in the ability to change is courage. Courage is not lack of fear. It is taking action in spite of fear. It is being willing to risk failure or exposure. Many people are so immobilized by fear of failure that they live timid, cautious lives. They cannot act because they are so afraid of what will happen if they fail. If you want to develop courage, give yourself permission to fail. Courage gives you the freedom to try.

Accept Your Limitations

While believing you can change is essential to actually doing so, it is not a magic answer. There are some things you can't change. You probably can't change the way your body responds to mood-altering substances when you ingest them. You probably can't change the way you metabolize alcohol when you drink. You can't change yourself into a 6'5" person if you are at your adult height of 5'4". There are some things that *just are*. When you can't accept some things as they are you are always going to be frustrated. You will expend energy on things you have no power over, neglecting things you do have the power to change.

Anxiety can occur when you do not accept your limitations, when you fail to acknowledge that there are some problems you can't solve. The limitations that reality puts on us can be stressful. We cannot always be perfect. We cannot always be the best.

Mistakes are not failure. They're just mistakes. A mistake is not failure unless you refuse to learn from it. If you look at a mistake as an opportunity to learn rather than as failure, it can just be a step in your success. Most of us learn as much from what we do wrong as from what we do right. We learn what works and what doesn't work. We learn what to do differently the next time. Seeing mistakes as steps in the learning process allows us to use them as assets.

Applying the Serenity Prayer

Wisdom for recovery lies in the words of the Serenity Prayer:

"God grant me the serenity to accept the things I cannot change, courage to change things I can, and wisdom to know the difference."

Before you develop the serenity of acceptance or the courage to change, it is necessary to learn to tell the difference.

Learning about chemical dependency and recovery will help you make responsible choices in relation to your condition. Numerous mistaken beliefs about chemical dependency can lead to trying to change what you are powerless over. When you learn that abstinence symptoms can be reduced by reducing stress, you can take action to change some stressful situations in life. The more you learn about addiction the better able you'll be to make responsible choices.

With the process of recovery, there is the growing realization that the freedom to choose comes with continued sobriety. You are free to change your own behavior; mind-altering chemicals are no longer making your choices. With the freedom to choose comes responsibility. You are free to make responsible choices.

You will find some things standing in the way of responsible behavior. But changing means taking risks. It takes courage to risk. It takes courage to change. You may make some mistakes along the way, but that's how you learn what works and what doesn't.

We create our own serenity by our attitudes and our spiritual resources. Serenity is a choice. You can fret about what you do not have the power to change—your heredity, the weather, what is in the past, what isn't here yet, other people. Or you can accept those things and reinvest that energy in what you do have the power to control. Serenity is accepting what is and setting yourself free—joyfully—to experience the gift of life and the pleasures of sobriety.

Serenity does not mean you don't have any unpleasant feelings. It means you accept life as it is and do not expend excessive energy fighting against what you are powerless over. It does not mean that you do not get angry or afraid. Serenity means accepting and acknowledging all of your feelings. It is knowing that if you get angry you can handle it without hurting yourself or others. You can be serene and still be sad when your dog dies. Serenity is acceptance that your feelings are valid so you don't have to be ashamed or feel guilty about them.

Serenity is also knowing that what you feel and what you do about your feelings are not the same thing. You can be afraid and not run from what you are afraid of. You can be angry and not become violent. You can be sad and not give up on life. You can learn ways to express your feelings that are appropriate and healing.

Perhaps the real secret of serenity is in living in the present—being present in the moment. There is little serenity in replaying what has already happened or waiting for some time in the future to enjoy life. If you are living for tomorrow you are missing out on today. Serenity increases as the experience of being present and comfortable in the moment increases.

"One day at a time" is a slogan learned in AA that is helpful in recovery because it teaches one to focus on the present. Sometimes it can be broken down to "one moment at a time." *Now* is all you have. The past is gone. You cannot change it. The future is not here yet. You cannot experience it. *The present is where life is lived.* Trying to live in the past or future robs you of the only life you have—the present.

CHAPTER 14

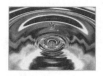

Enriching Life

WE ALL HAVE a need for harmony in our lives. While struggling
with addiction, your life may have become chaotic and unpre-
dictable. At times you may have felt the insecurity of living on
the edge—the edge of despair, the edge of giving up, the edge of
complete loss of control. You may have felt the impact physically, mentally, emotionally, socially, and spiritually. You may
have been out of harmony with yourself, others, and the world.

When we are focused on drinking or not drinking, we are
out of balance, trying to do the impossible. Like a top that
can't spin when it is not evenly weighted, we are drained of
energy by our efforts to keep an unbalanced life in motion.
When we are not getting as much energy from life as it drains
from us, we are out of balance.

Balance creates energy; as we grow in recovery, we revital-
ize and rebalance all areas of our lives. We are released from
attempting to achieve unattainable goals. Sickness and dishar-
mony are replaced with wholeness and balance. We are revi-

talized, reconnected with healthy living. When we are living a balanced life, we are living responsibly, with time for family, job, friends, and ourselves. Balanced living includes attention to health care with proper focus on nutrition, exercise, and rest; attention to personal growth with proper regard to attitudes, feelings, and actions; a healthy social network; and enriching spiritual life.

At first, recovery may seem chaotic. So much focus and attention on self-care may seem to put your life even more out of balance. It may seem that you are adding to an already-too-full schedule of activities, causing you to neglect other things that are important. But you cannot integrate good self-care into a balanced life until you learn the basic how-to's. Unavoidably, even in a life that is well balanced, special needs will arise that will cause you to focus on one aspect of living to the temporary exclusion of others. Beginning recovery is such a time. Learning good self-care habits and putting them into practice take time and energy, it's true, but after a while these practices become a predictable part of life.

As recovery becomes "normal," you can move beyond basic self-care requirements—eating routines, exercise plans, and meetings. You can expand recovery. You will come to know yourself better while you become aware of the balance between too much and too little stress, responsibility to yourself and to others, time for work and time for play, time for activity and time for rest.

Balance of Body, Mind, and Spirit

We cannot look to any one aspect of life for all the answers. Because we are composed of many parts, we derive strength from many sources. Balanced living means we are healthy physically and psychologically and have healthy relationships.

We recognize that each part of our lives impacts the others. We are no longer focused on only one aspect of life. We strive for and are motivated toward wholesome living.

Physical health allows psychological growth: When we feel good, we find it is easier to think about our attitudes and values and to work on eliminating shame, guilt, and anger. Psychological health allows us to do more easily those things that keep our bodies well. Healthy relationships support our personal growth.

But the whole is more than the sum of the parts. There is something more that is part of a whole person. Let's call it spirit. The spirit is more than just another part. It includes body, mind, feelings, behavior, and relationships, and it joins them all into a whole. The parts cannot be healthy until the whole is.

Balance Between Work and Play

Life is learning, and we learn better when we are having fun. For too many of us, fun is what we do when all the serious stuff (work) is done. Thinking this way keeps us imprisoned in the belief that we can "live" only on the weekends, on vacation, in retirement, or when we win the lottery.

Children do not make a distinction between work and play, they just experience life. Most adults have lost that ability. To the extent that we can recapture it, we allow ourselves to enjoy whatever we are doing, whatever we call it. Of course, we can't eliminate all activities that we do not especially enjoy; some tasks will resist being transformed from travail into treat. That is part of life. But it is still possible to enjoy a sense of accomplishment for doing them and to appreciate what we learn from the experience—and equally important to give ourselves opportunity for the activities we do enjoy.

Balance Between Relaxation and Stimulation

Sometimes an unbalanced life means we need to learn to take life easier; sometimes it means we need more activities that stimulate and invigorate us. Rest is not doing nothing; it is enjoying the freedom to do anything.

We can be re-energized through both activity and inactivity. Research indicates that we need a balance of brain chemicals that stimulate us and those that calm us down. Some people prefer activities that produce "upper" chemistry; others tend to go for a "downer" chemistry. Both types of activity do promote feelings of well-being. But while all of us have our preference, most of us need some mixture of both types in order to live harmoniously with ourselves.

In recovery we may need to find new ways to feel calm or stimulated. Watching television or reading are good calming activities, but relaxation usually needs to be balanced by some activities that are physically stimulating (such as dancing) or mentally stimulating (playing a game or engaging in meaningful conversation). Relaxing means more than putting our feet up, although it certainly includes giving ourselves permission to do that. It also means experiencing stimulation.

The balance of inactivity and activity also produces a balance of certain types of brain waves. When we are active, especially mentally active, we usually produce beta brain waves. When we are more mentally relaxed, we experience alpha and theta waves. Deep concentration produces a beta state; relaxation exercises produce an alpha or theta state. All mental states are essential to our total well-being, spending an inordinate amount of time in any one creates an imbalance. We create balance with variety in our activities.

Balance Between Giving and Receiving

For many of us, the most difficult aspect of our lives to balance is fulfilling our responsibility to ourselves and our responsibility to others. Placing care of ourselves high on our list of priorities does not mean we do not also care for other people. Nor does giving to other people, even sacrificing for them, mean we should neglect our own recovery or our own growth. When we love ourselves, we take care of ourselves. When we love others, we allow them to take responsibility for their own lives as much as possible—but we support their growth, in whatever ways we can, without damaging ourselves.

As with other areas of recovery, our ability to provide for our own needs while responding to the needs of others expands as our recovery skills increase. At first, we may need to concentrate on our own needs as we learn to implement components of a self-care program. As those activities become a normal part of life, we are able to become more involved in supporting someone else. Paradoxically, giving often comes back to us as a gift.

As her recovery expanded, Marilyn found that giving to others benefited her own growth. She put up in her car a little sign that read PASS IT ON, and often took people who did not have transportation to the doctor, or the grocery store, or to AA meetings. She found time to listen when others needed someone to talk to. When anyone asked her what they could do to repay her, she said, "Pass it on." Recently while a friend was in her home, Marilyn mentioned that she was unable to repaint her woodwork because she was allergic to the paint fumes. The friend said, "I'll paint your woodwork while you are on vacation and will air out your house before you get back." Marilyn was deeply touched that someone would offer to do that for her. The friend, seeing Marilyn's reaction, said, "I'm just passing it on."

When we pass it on, we build a sense of community. When we just repay what has been done for us, we only balance the scales. The world is a better place to be when we are passing it on. A new energy is created that keeps on giving.

We need other people; our growth is dependent upon them. At the same time, we need to give to other people. We need to be concerned about others and contribute to their well-being. Through interaction with others we give and receive the feedback necessary for continuing growth. We cannot grow in a vacuum.

Many of us have not been able to achieve the balance of giving and receiving because we do not know how to love ourselves. Those of us who have lived in shame, who have felt defective and unacceptable, may feel unworthy of love and acceptance from others or from ourselves. When our recovery enables us to accept ourselves as we are, we are better able to have mutually supportive relationships with others.

We need strong social networks to nurture us and provide a sense of belonging. We need reciprocal relationships in which we feel valued as we value others, and experience the satisfaction of giving and receiving.

Spiritual Balance

Spiritual balance means we are in harmony with ourselves, with our values, with others, and with God. Step Eleven of AA gives us guidance for achieving spiritual balance: "Sought through prayer and meditation to improve our conscious contact with God as we understood him, praying only for knowledge of His will for us and the power to carry that out." Just as we don't have to have any special concept of God to do this, neither do we have to use any certain definition of prayer or meditation.

But this step is not about trying to get our higher power to do what we want. It is about aligning our will with a higher will. It is about getting in touch with a power that will help us increase our understanding, our knowledge, our courage, and our willingness to live wholesome lives.

"Prayer does not change God, but changes him who prays."

Soren Kierkegaard

Spiritual wholeness is living in harmony with what we believe and value. Shame and guilt result from lack of harmony between our values and our behavior. Conscious contact with a higher power, increased knowledge of that power's will for us, and the power to carry that out enable us to find harmony between what we believe and what we do. We are thus freed from the burden of guilt and shame to find spiritual fulfillment.

Living in balance does not mean we do not have bad days. We still have our ups and downs; we still experience sadness, anger, fatigue, disappointment. We accept these feelings when they are appropriate. We don't have to be ashamed of them or feel guilty for having them. We allow ourselves to experience a whole range of feelings, but we don't let them control us. And we know how to take action that will prevent these emotions from triggering regression. A wholesome, harmonious life does not mean we never do things we regret or feel bad about. It means that we don't need to become discouraged by our inability to be perfect.

When we are living in balance, we accept our humanness and strive for progress. We seek to eliminate activities that cause us to go to extremes at the expense of other important parts of life. We give up the need for immediate gratification in order to achieve a lifestyle that is more fulfilling and meaningful.

Joyful Living

Is there a voice within you, calling you to dream and to believe in your dreams? Listen to that voice. It is your creative spirit. It is calling you to live fully and passionately, to risk and to play. It is calling you to joy. As you listen to that voice and respond to it, it will become stronger. It is calling you to see yourself as a person of integrity and worth, one who has unique dreams and unique talents to offer the world. Responding to that special call leads us on a journey that goes beyond preventing relapse, beyond just getting back to ground zero. Seeing the possibilities of life and seeing ourselves with the potential for attaining wholeness gives purpose and meaning to our journey. That sense of purpose and meaning is a result and a facilitator of healing.

Replacing self-defeating lifestyles with hope and meaning takes self-care beyond maintenance into abundant living. Abundant living means more than material abundance. It means lives that are rich physically, mentally, socially, and spiritually. Moving beyond the issues of using or not using, we replace artificial ways of feeling good with natural ways. The brain creates positive chemistry and generates positive thoughts and feelings, leading to an expectation of opportunities and new possibilities. Life becomes an adventure.

We do not become aware of the possibilities for abundance if our main interest in life is the prevention of relapse. If we don't see something bright and new to move into, we can only long for what we are giving up. If we focus on an abundant life, and stay focused on it, then we will hope for that abundance, expect it, and seek it. If we feed our hopes, our fears will starve to death.

People who don't know how to live fully use temporary, artificial substitutes for the real riches that life offers. But we know that in the long run these substitutes only increase pain, deadening senses rather than awakening them.

People who have used addictive living to produce pleasure or relieve pain and who don't know any other way to feel good or to relieve their pain, will eventually go back to addictive use. If our emphasis is on not drinking, then we're focused on what we are not doing; we're saying no to life. It is time we say "yes"—yes to living fully and joyfully.

A Spiritual Awakening

Step Twelve of AA says, *"Having had a spiritual awakening as a result of these steps, we tried to carry this message to others and to practice these principles in all our affairs."* A spiritual awakening occurs as we go beyond the struggle of controlling our addiction and, having found meaning beyond ourselves, we discover the joys of living. We experience enriching pleasures that take us beyond just "not using." We actively participate in life rather than passively hoping life will offer us something good along the way.

A spiritual awakening occurs as we learn that spirituality is not separate from our daily lives, but encompasses life and brings new meaning to all our affairs. Although spirituality must be defined by each of us for ourselves alone, it is interesting to note that *Webster's Dictionary* tells us the word is derived from *spiritus*, which means "of breathing" and "an animating or vital principle held to give life. . . ." Our spiritual awakening allows this animating force to be breathed into all areas of our existence.

Spirituality and religion are not the same thing. Religion is a set of beliefs about the spiritual and the practices based on those beliefs. Religion certainly is a means by which some people connect to the spiritual, but we may experience a spiritual awakening without being affiliated with a specific religion or religious denomination. A spiritual awakening is a personal experience that opens the door to meaningful and creative living.

Living Creatively

When creativity is blocked, the result is powerlessness and impotence. To live creatively is to give expression to our inner selves. A creative spirit calls us to create laughter, love, forgiveness, and healing in ourselves and others. Creativity may be expressed through cooking, gardening, caring for children, caring for elderly, writing, playing, making love, decorating, painting, dancing, journaling, teaching, counseling, repairing, designing, and so on.

The call to creativity is a call to joy, zest, and a sense of meaning and purpose. Are you listening to that call? Failure to experience life's meaningful pleasures creates a void that is often filled with destructive "pleasures." They offer no hope and no joy.

We need to sharpen our senses rather than deaden them. We need to wake up and see what is already around us. Someone has said boredom comes from lack of involvement. Get involved. Celebrate life. Celebrate people and animals and all creation. Celebrate yourself.

"We must learn to reawaken and keep ourselves awake, not by mechanical aids, but by an infinite expectation of the dawn, which does not forsake us in our soundest sleep."

Henry David Thoreau

To live creatively and joyfully does not mean being happy all the time. Struggle is a normal and usually necessary part of creativity, just as labor is a normal part of giving birth. To live joyfully is to experience a fullness of life; it is to be open to suffering as well as to pleasure. Pain is woven into life's pleasures and comforts, and is even essential to them. When we turn away from struggle, we turn away from progress, and a deeper pain grows. To escape from normal pain and struggle is to escape from life.

Compassion

Our pain can never be erased without compassion—"an awakening of passion with all creation."[1] Compassionate living means maintaining creative relationships with the earth, the creatures of the earth, and other people. The reason we damage the earth, one another, and ourselves is that we are out of harmony. Harmony results from valuing all creation, including ourselves—our bodies, minds, and spirits. Destructiveness comes from not honoring life. Compassion is reverence for life, including a reverence for our own specialness and our own beauty.

"The most beautiful experience we can have is the mysterious. It is the fundamental emotion which stands at the cradle of true art and true science. Whoever does not know it and can no longer wonder, no longer marvel, is as good as dead."

Albert Einstein

Compassion brings responsibility, not out of prim "duty," but out of our wanting to care for what we cherish and value. What do you cherish? What are you enthusiastic about? The word enthusiasm means "spirit." Do you have life-spirit? Do you have self-spirit? Compassion is a call to courage. Discouragement kills faith and hope and spirit. Courage awakens and empowers. It empowers us to walk into our dreams with hope and enthusiasm.

An important aspect of recovery is giving to others out of compassion and concern. Our own wounds become a resource for healing—out of our suffering come the wisdom and understanding to pass the healing on. Those of us for whom addiction has been the object and focus of life have the opportunity to give to others in recovery. Having lived through much anguish, we are survivors of a condition that has eaten the very center out of our self-esteem. Out of this struggle, we gain insight and compassion to give to and receive from others. Sharing these principles with others is important in keeping them active in our own lives.

"Nothing renews commitment like sharing the joy that results from the commitment . . . sharing keeps the light on and the spirit high."

Larrene Hagaman[2]

Sharing with others keeps the growth process going. Without it, we retreat back into ourselves and allow the old shames to creep in and take over. "Carrying the message" allows life to take on an "other" focus rather than just a "self" focus. As we give to others, we reflect their worth and see our own worth reflected in them. This sense of unity creates a deeper sense of the interconnectedness we have with others and with all living things.

Freedom

Freedom of choice is the greatest opportunity we have. We can choose life; we can choose to take a different path no matter where we have been. We can choose to use the resources we have to become what we were created to be. Or we can choose to hang on to feelings of inadequacy that keep us locked into discouragement.

As we become aware of our ability to use our own judgment and, through that exercise, to assert more control over our own lives, we begin to see our potential instead of our shortcomings. We stop seeing other people through defensive eyes as we learn to see them in the light of our empowering interaction with them. We see that we, as individuals working and playing together, can become more than we could in isolation.

We really do not grow or gain in self-esteem by adhering to the wisdom of the self alone. We need, ultimately, to feel a sense of belonging. We need to be involved with others, to exchange perceptions with them, to give and get support. We need others to help us stop the inner war that is fueled by shame and distorted pictures of ourselves.

Freedom comes from an emphasis on what we are seeking rather than on what we are avoiding. If emphasis is on the not (what we are not consuming, what habits we are not engaging in), then we are always aware of what is lacking in our lives. Life seems to mean deprivation and restriction. But as we move into replacement activities our picture of life changes:

We see and we expect abundance. Harmony in all aspects of life allows us the balance to go beyond the struggle of using drugs, and to enter into the experience of joyful living. We reach for an enriched life that is full physically, mentally, emotionally, socially, and spiritually. Armed, as never before against regression, we spiral up now, into new aspects of growth.

Serendipity

A bonus on the recovery journey, serendipity is the good fortune of discovering something good while seeking something else. It happens when we compare what we have been seeking with what we have found, and decide that the thing we've found is even better than that which we'd sought. Many people, out of their pain and acceptance, have experiences in which their insights and benefits far surpass their expectations of merely staying on track.

The person at an AA meeting who says "I'm a grateful alcoholic" is describing this experience of serendipity. She has found on her healing journey much more than she ever expected, more than only maintaining abstinence, more than "just hanging on." A new way of life has opened up for her. Expecting serendipity means living in a way that says, "Today I can experience only the present. As I do, I expect the unexpected. I have a choice to truly experience today, as fully as I can."

A certain story has held particular meaning for us, and we wish to share it with you. We hope it will help light the path that you take in recovery.

There was once a young farm boy whose father was away and whose mother asked him to go to the barn in the dark to feed the animals. But he was afraid of the dark. His mother assured him that the lantern would furnish the light he needed to get there and back. "But the lantern only shines its light a short way in front of me," he said. "I can't see all the way to the barn." Then, handing him the lantern, his mother took him outside. "Now, Son," she said, "just take one step toward the barn." As he took one step the light moved ahead of him. "All you have to do," his mother told him, "is take one step at a time and the light will go before you all the way."

There is a light that goes ahead of us on our recovery journey. We can see as far as we need to see to live a full and joyful life. We don't have to wait until we get to the end of the journey to begin living or to experience the light. As you take your next steps into recovery, watch for the light that illuminates your path.

Putting It All Together

Bridging the Gaps

BRIDGING THE GAPS, INC., located in Winchester, Virginia, was founded by Stanley Stokes for the purpose of providing a physiological/biochemical rebalancing approach to addiction recovery. Stan was motivated to find integrative methods for more effective treatment by the high rate of relapse he saw with traditional treatment and, more recently, with the use of prescription medications.

Bridging the Gaps was established to do just that: bridge the gaps between what was being done in treatment and what he believed was possible with biochemical rebalancing. This process of rebalancing the brain chemistry is a model in progress at BTG. BTG is combining knowledge from credentialed colleagues and consultants to develop a well founded and rounded program. Dr. Charles Gant, Dr. James Braly, David Miller, Merlene Miller, and Julia Ross are consultants to the program and provide training and guidance in amino acid therapy (both intravenous and oral), nutritional counseling, client education, and relapse prevention.

The unique programs at BTG focus on an integrated approach to the physiological rebalancing as well as the psychological, emotional, spiritual and social facets of recovery. The programs incorporate many treatment modalities including intravenous nutritional therapy, oral nutrient therapy, acu-detox, nutritional counseling, physical exercise, massage, Reiki, and yoga, to aide an individual's health recovery. Brainwave biofeedback is also available. In addition, all programs are enhanced with a relapse prevention skills training program developed by Merlene and David Miller.

By adhering to a program of healthy eating habits, structured daily exercise, meditation, relaxation, and restful sleep, the recovering individual will be much better equipped to stay sober. Having re-balanced brain chemistry and identified warning signs, triggers, and high risk situations in a real life setting and actively participated in a 12-Step program, the recovering resident will enjoy the encouragement and support needed to make the transition to sober living.

The spirit of Bridging the Gaps is captured in this writing by Dr. Ben:

The BTG Spirit

"We are here because in the end there is no refuge from ourselves. Until we confront ourselves in the eyes and hearts of others, we are merely running. Until we share our secrets, we have no safety from them. Afraid to be known, we can know neither ourselves nor any other—we are alone. Where else but in our common ground can we find such a mirror? Here, together, we can at last appear clearly to ourselves—not as the giants of our dreams or the dwarfs of our fears—but as individual parts of a whole, with a share in its future. In this place, we can each take root and grow, not alone anymore as in death, but alive to ourselves and others . . . to finally serve a higher purpose."

The Recovery Systems Clinic

Julia Ross, M.A., is founder and executive director of Recovery Systems in Mill Valley, California, which provides holistic outpatient assessments, counseling and nutritional therapy along with medical care for alcohol, drug and food addictions. Ross is also the author of *The Diet Cure* and *The Mood Cure.* Her staff of holistic nutritionists, counselors, and physicians are trained by Ross to identify symptoms of neu-rotransmitter deficiencies as well as other nutritional deficien-cies, and to provide appropriate treatment for the deficiencies and their underlying causes.

The program starts with a bio-psycho-social assessment (in person only), for individuals (and their families, when possi-ble) to explore issues contributing to addictive cravings. The first appointment lasts four or five hours in order to provide in-depth understanding and treatment of the health issues and history that have caused the person to seek help. Recommendations for testing are made. Then a comprehensive treatment plan is designed, including appropriate individual, family, group and educational counseling, as well as peer sup-port. When residential treatment is needed Recovery Systems personnel work closely with associated facilities.

Nutritional therapy provides a pro-recovery diet and target-ed nutritional supplement protocols. In-office trials of oral amino acids are provided. The initial session is followed by weekly appointments for at least three months (by phone or in person). Oral amino acids—as part of a total nutritional pro-gram—are an important part of the treatment recommended to relieve cravings and "false moods." Medical care is provided in the way of examinations, special testing, and prescriptions, as needed.

Intravenous amino acid therapy is available through Recovery Systems when determined advisable, especially for detoxification from mood-altering substances. Withdrawal from benzodiazapine medications is a specialty of the program. Out-of-towners can take their individualized IV formula to a medical doctor in their local area for further treatments, if needed, after they have had at least a few IV sessions at Recovery Systems.

The Power Recovery Program

This is a consulting program based on the experience and scientific research of Charles Gant, M.D., Ph.D, N.M.D. The service is based on the premise that substance abuse problems are the result of biochemical imbalances that disrupt the normal workings of brain cells. Information is gathered through a questionnaire process or with personal assessment by Dr. Gant. Products (Relax Pak, Lift Pak, Tobac Pak, or Detox Pak) are recommended according to the brain chemistry imbalances indicated. Supplements come in a thirty-day supply of sixty individually wrapped packets. The supplement "paks" are based on the research reported in the book *End Your Addiction Now* by Dr. Gant, and are made up of the appropriate combination of amino acids, vitamins, and minerals. Using the nutrient "paks" can help restore neurotransmitter production by supplying the brain with the raw materials needed to rebalance chemistry.

Excel Treatment

Excel is an outpatient addiction treatment program located in Denver, Colorado, and was founded by Dr. Tamea Sisco, a chiropractor and certified addictionologist. She began using intravenous nutraceuticals because it made so much sense in light of what she knew about addiction and the brain. The treatment philosophy at Excel is based on research that shows that the cause and treatment for addiction centers on the brain—not just in the mind. At Excel clients are taught that addiction results from a genetic brain disorder that causes dopamine receptor sites to be in short supply. Substances such as alcohol and other drugs destroy more dopamine receptor sites creating a need for an ever-increasing consumption of the substance and discomfort when the substance is not present in the body.

Treatment at Excel features intravenous and oral mixes of amino acids, peptides, vitamins, and minerals, and help reverse the genetic and drug related damage, thereby boosting the brain's ability to absorb dopamine. The intravenous therapy is administered under the supervision of a licensed physician for ten days. It is administered as a painless drip over three or four hours for ten treatments, and is followed by monthly follow-up treatment for six months. While it has consistently produced dramatic results in reversing physiological addictions, a comprehensive psychological counseling program is also implemented; such a program supports the continuation of a new lifestyle that is important to long-term success.

Excel claims a greater than 80 percent success rate over a period of twelve months. Dr. Thomas Levy, medical director of Excel says, "We have now been administering the IV treatment for all types of addictive behavior with incredible success." He reports that patients experience no cravings and no withdrawal symptoms. Dr. Sisco adds that safety is important; thus, all amino acids used are FDA approved.

In addition to psychological counseling, other modalities such as acupuncture, massage, and ionic foot baths are used to enhance the effectiveness of treatment at Excel. In 2005, Excel will open a hospital-based inpatient program that will provide additional services including a relapse prevention program utilizing materials developed by Merlene and David Miller.

At Excel you are apt to hear someone say, "It's time to treat addiction with both brain- and mind-based therapy because it is all in your head."

Community Addiction Recovery Association

Community Addiction Recovery Association (CARA) is a nonprofit organization in Sacramento, California, treating chemical dependency with acupuncture, herbal tea, yoga, nutritional supplements, nutrition education, Chinese exercise routines (tai qi and qi gong), and emotional freedom technique, a uniquely successful method of relieving post traumatic stress and other emotionally charged memories through verbalization of the problem coupled with acupressure. Staff includes licensed acupuncturists and certified practitioners of clinical nutrition and the various mind-body integration techniques offered.

CARA contracts with individual treatment facilities to provide any or all of these services on site. Each facility chooses the programs they desire from the spectrum available. For example, longstanding contracts include a one-hour acupuncture session per week for early recovery patients in Kaiser Permanente's Chemical Dependency Recovery Program, while early recovery clients at Sacramento County's drug court receive daily acupuncture plus weekly sessions of all the other above mentioned protocols for the first three months of their 10-16 month program.

CARA uses the standard National Acupuncture Detoxification Association's five-point ear treatment, including sites for relaxing the sympathetic nervous system, improving the function of kidneys, liver, and lungs, and releasing mood elevating endorphins.

Inspired by the Radiant Recovery program of Kathleen DesMaisons, Ph.D. (now located in Albuquerque, New Mexico), CARA provides a protein beverage each morning consisting of frozen fruit, fruit juice, powdered nutrients, and protein powder.

Clients write down what they eat and drink each day, the time they eat it, various feelings they notice, and the time they notice them. Once a week a nutritionist goes over the journal individually with clients and helps each form a goal for the next week (i.e. "Eat a green or red vegetable each day." or "Drink more water."). The purpose is for clients to learn from the patterns they see in their eating or not eating. What made them feel calm and happy, and what led to using drugs, angry outbursts, and depression? How different did they feel after three nutritious meals versus their usual fasting/junk food routine?

In August 2002, CARA added what they think is the most important component, individualized amino acids based on the protocol of Joan Mathews Larson, described in her books *Seven Weeks to Sobriety* and *Depression-Free, Naturally*. In addition, CARA's work is enhanced by direct advice from Julia Ross, author of *The Diet Cure* and *The Mood Cure*.

Exercise allows drug abusers to be re-introduced to their bodies and in the process learn a simple method of stress reduction. The gentle, flowing exercise called tai qi is easy for pregnant or obese women. Qi gong teaches power over breath and body for self-mastery and healing. Yoga integrates mind and body through control of breath, mind, and body. Clients are often emotionally fragile, physically damaged, with short attention spans. These forms of self-healing don't need a lot of intellectual discussion. They are viscerally satisfying even to those who aren't ready for or are resisting talk therapy.

Future plans include a newsletter and educational materials introducing both acupuncture and targeted nutrition to the recovery community.

Counseling and Mediation Services

Carol Cummings, M.S.W., an addiction counselor in private practice as part of Counseling and Mediation Services in Wichita, Kansas, uses a variety of alternative treatment methods. First, the client is assessed, usually by a psychiatrist, to evaluate any serotonin or dopamine deficit or other neurochemical imbalance. Appropriate amino acid supplements and vitamins are then recommended. Clients are introduced to a variety of stress-reducing techniques including slowing breath, progressive relaxation, meditation, prayer, music, and art.

Clients are introduced to aromatherapy to enhance stress reduction and promote wellness. Aromas seem to work by bypassing walls of defenses and affecting the brain directly through the olfactory nerve. Pure essence oils are used because very few people are allergic to them. One of the most popular is a combination of oils called Peace and Calming, which reduces depression and cravings. Sandalwood is used to aid recovery from co-dependency and adjustment disorders. Color therapy is utilized when appropriate. For example, yellow is used to help heal the pancreas.

Cummings incorporates a variety of bi-lateral stimulation exercises to help reduce trauma (due to the physical abuse, sexual abuse, chaotic families, accidents, etc., often experienced by addicts) and enhance healing of the brain. She teaches an exercise routine to be used every morning.

The routine begins by drinking eight ounces of water to increase energy by increasing electrical potential across membranes and increasing oxygen uptake. Next, spots located around carotid arteries underneath the collar bone are masssaged, while placing one hand on the navel. This supplies fresh oxygenated blood to the brain.

All of this is followed by a cross crawl exercise that is like a very slow march: stand, lift right leg, put left hand on right knee. Put down the right knee and then lift the left knee, right hand on knee. Done slowly, this activates both hemispheres of the brain.

The next exercise is called hook-ups: cross legs at ankles, extend arms in front, bring backs of hands together, thumbs pointing down, cross hands over, interlace fingers, bring arms to chest, bend elbows and breathe, relax into it. This posture reduces anxiety and stress. It activates sensory and motor cortexes in both hemispheres of the cerebrum simultaneously. While doing this, place the tongue on the roof of the mouth. The tongue connects the limbic and frontal lobes of the brain.

This exercise routine increases oxygen amount and flow to the brain, increases and balances electrical energy to the neocortex, moving it away from the survival centers in the brain stem. This allows choice by providing access to reason rather than reaction and increases polarity across cell membranes, for more efficient thought processing and focused attention.

The individual parts of this exercise routine can be used throughout the day whenever needed. In addition, Cummings teaches a variety of techniques to be used as needed to reduce any pain, stress, anxiety or cravings.

Classical music (especially Mozart) works directly on the brain for relaxation, healing, learning, and enhancing creativity. It can be used to attain an altered state of awareness and allows deep healing of the brain. Cummings recommends that music and other meditation exercises be followed by drawing images that describe what the experience was like and that bring it into conscious awareness to reinforce it.

Serotonin Deficiency Questionnaire

The following questions, developed by James Braly, M.D., can help determine your brain serotonin status and whether or not you are serotonin deficient.

Circle the number that best represents your condition, using the following scale.

> 0 = never, don't know
> 1 = occasionally, but not severe
> 2 = occasionally and severe
> 3 = frequently, but not severe
> 4 = frequently and severe

1) Irritable?	0	1	2	3	4
2) Agitated, flustered, angry and/or upset?	0	1	2	3	4
3) Temper tantrums/quick temper?	0	1	2	3	4
4) Throw things/hit walls when upset?	0	1	2	3	4

5) Antisocial feelings or tendencies? 0 1 2 3 4

6) Fear that you will say or do something that will
 embarrass or humiliate yourself when with others? 0 1 2 3 4

7) Fear that others will notice that you are nervous? 0 1 2 3 4

8) Typically avoid speaking to small groups or
 chatting over lunch with friends or associates? 0 1 2 3 4

9) Intense distress or anxiousness when speaking
 to small groups? 0 1 2 3 4

10) Impulsive, outward aggressiveness? 0 1 2 3 4

11) Ever cruel to animals? 0 1 2 3 4

12) Have been in at least one physical fight since
 you were 18 years old? 0 1 2 3 4

13) Impatient, given to acting impulsively? 0 1 2 3 4

14) Physical risk taking? 0 1 2 3 4

15) Psychological stress? 0 1 2 3 4

16) Do not handle stress well? 0 1 2 3 4

17) Anxious, nervous? 0 1 2 3 4

18) Panic attacks? 0 1 2 3 4

19) Moody, highly changeable moods? 0 1 2 3 4

20) Suffer from frequent depression or sadness
 for no apparent reason? 0 1 2 3 4

21) Intentionally injure or physically hurt yourself? 0 1 2 3 4

22) Felt suicidal at different times in your life? 0 1 2 3 4

23) Have disagreeable thoughts or impulses that
 you have trouble controlling? 0 1 2 3 4

24) Very sensitive to criticism, disapproval or rejection? 0 1 2 3 4

25) Hypersensitive to the anger and sadness you feel? 0 1 2 3 4

26) Insomnia, restless sleep, frequent awakenings? 0 1 2 3 4

27) Have a "night owl" pattern of sleep (prefer
 later bedtime)? 0 1 2 3 4

28) Tend to be overly dependent in significant
 relationships? 0 1 2 3 4

29) Over-consumption of alcohol, tendency towards
 alcohol abuse? 0 1 2 3 4

30) Alcohol cravings, especially after hard day's
work or periods of stress?   0   1   2   3   4

31) When consuming alcohol, difficulty limiting
yourself to only one or two drinks?   0   1   2   3   4

32) Anger, aggressiveness and/or violence when drinking?   0   1   2   3   4

33) "Fearlessness" after a few alcoholic drinks?   0   1   2   3   4

34) Smoke cigarettes or cigars daily?   0   1   2   3   4

35) Sweat less than most people?   0   1   2   3   4

36) Engage in binge eating?   0   1   2   3   4

37) Binge on large quantities of food, and then
purge food by vomiting?   0   1   2   3   4

38) Crave carbohydrates, sweets and/or chocolate?   0   1   2   3   4

39) Think about food a lot and overeat?   0   1   2   3   4

40) Suffer from anorexia nervosa or other
"eating disorders"?   0   1   2   3   4

41) Suffer from symptoms of low blood sugar
or hypoglycemia?   0   1   2   3   4

42) Strong craving or preference for fatty foods?   0   1   2   3   4

43) Taking appetite-suppressing medication
to lose weight?   0   1   2   3   4

44) On a low fat, low cholesterol diet?   0   1   2   3   4

45) Presently taking a cholesterol-lowering medication?   0   1   2   3   4

46) Have very low blood total cholesterol
(under 150 mg/dL)?   0   1   2   3   4

47) Suffer from a chronic inflammatory bowel or
intestinal disease (Crohn's disease,
ulcerative colitis, chronic diarrhea)?   0   1   2   3   4

48) Suffer from gluten cereal (wheat, rye) sensitivity
or celiac disease?   0   1   2   3   4

49) Overweight, excessively fat?   0   1   2   3   4

50) Feel noticeably better on sunny days and/or
worse under conditions of light deprivation
(e.g., overcast, winter days)?   0   1   2   3   4

51) Have a low tolerance for heat?   0   1   2   3   4

52) Have chronic pain for more than 3 months duration?　0　1　2　3　4

53) Suffer from recurring migraine headaches?　　　　　0　1　2　3　4

54) Suffer from fibromyalgia (tender spots on muscles
　　of neck, shoulders, back, hips, and/or legs
　　associated with fatigue, sleep disorder, rhinitis)?　0　1　2　3　4

55) Have significantly more frequent sex or sexual
　　partners than is usual among your peers?　　　　0　1　2　3　4

56) Suffer from curvature of the spine (scoliosis)?　　0　1　2　3　4

FOR MEN ONLY:

57) Suffer from premature ejaculation during
　　sexual intercourse?　　　　　　　　　　　　　0　1　2　3　4

FOR WOMEN ONLY:

58) Suffer from premenstrual syndrome?　　　　　　0　1　2　3　4

59) Suffer from depression, anxiety, sugar cravings
　　around period?　　　　　　　　　　　　　　　0　1　2　3　4

Total Score　=　_____

If your score exceeds 30, you may be suffering from significant serotonin deficiency, and serotonin restoration therapy is indicated.

17 Proven Ways To Increase Brain Serotonin Levels— The Natural Way

1) Avoiding alcoholic beverages
2) Avoiding excess stimulants (including caffeinated drinks and cigarettes)
3) Exposure to bright light and/or sunlight 1-2 hours daily
4) Sixty minutes of moderate to moderately intense exercise daily
5) Deep, restful, snore-free sleep (stages III and IV sleep)

ORAL SUPPLEMENTATION:
6) 5-hydroxytryptophan (5-HTP)
7) Ginkgo biloba, 24% standardized
8) Acetyl-L carnitine (increases dopamine, serotonin and acetylcholine receptors and their release)
9) St. John's Wort, standardized
10) Vitamin B6, B12, folic acid and B2 with TMG (decreases plasma homocysteine, raising SAMe)
11) NADH (increases dopamine dramatically, serotonin less)
12) SAMe (S-adenosyl-methionine—activates CNS neurotransmitters, including serotonin)
13) Growth hormone-releasing amino acids such as arginine, ornithine, tyrosine & glutamine.
14) DHA-rich cod liver oil
15) Vitamin D (oral supplementation and/or direct sunlight on skin)

DIETARY
16) Identification and elimination of food allergens with special attention to gluten cereals and milk
17) Fish-rich diet (4-6 ounce un-fried, un-breaded servings, 3 days per week)

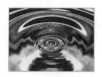

Glycemic Index

FOOD	GLYCEMIC INDEX (GLUCOSE = 100)
BAKERY PRODUCTS	
Muffins	
Apple made without sugar	48
Blueberry	59
Bran	60
Corn	49
Breads and pastry	
Bagel, plain, frozen	72
Croissant	67
Doughnut	76
Hamburger bun	61
Melba toast	70
Pita bread	57
Pumpernickel	41

Sourdough	52
Waffles	76
White bread	70
Whole wheat (100%)	51

Breakfast cereals

All-Bran	42
Corn Flakes	84
Grape-Nuts	67
Muesli	66
Nutri-grain	66
Puffed Wheat	74
Shredded Wheat	69

DAIRY

Ice cream	50
Skim milk	32
Yogurt	38

GRAINS

Barley	25
Bulgur (cracked wheat)	48
Couscous	65
Hominy	40
Oat bran, raw	55
Rice, brown	55
Rice, instant	91
Rice, white, low-amylose	88
Rice bran	19
Sweet corn	55

FRUITS

Apple	36
Apricots	57
Banana, ripe	52

Cantaloupe	65
Cherries	22
Grapefruit	25
Grapes	43
Kiwi	52
Orange	43
Peach	28
Pear	33
Pineapple	66
Plum	24
Raisins	64
Strawberries	32
Watermelon	72

LEGUMES

Baby limas	32
Baked beans	48
Black beans	30
Chickpeas	33
Kidney beans	27
Lentils	29
Navy beans	38
Pinto beans	42
Soybeans	18
Split peas	32

PASTA

Linguine	46
Macaroni and cheese, boxed	64
Spaghetti	41
Spaghetti, boiled 5 minutes (al dente)	37

SNACK FOODS AND CANDY

Corn chips	73

Jelly beans	80
Peanuts	14
Popcorn	55
Cookies	
Oatmeal	55
Shortbread	64
Vanilla wafer	77
Cakes	
Angel food cake	67
Pound cake	54
Sponge cake	46

VEGETABLES

Carrots	71
Peas, green	48
Potato, baked	85
Sweet corn	55
Sweet potato	54

Recipes

Bridging the Gaps

Chicken Teriyaki

1 c. Bragg liquid aminos
2 Tbsp. olive oil
3 scallions, chopped
2 Tbsp. honey
2 cloves garlic
3/4 c. water
1 tsp. ground ginger
juice of 1/2 lemon
1 large chicken, cut up

Combine ingredients, marinate chicken at least 2 hours. Grill or bake in moderate 350° oven until done (20-40 minutes). Test for doneness. If the juices are pink, it's raw; if the juices run clear, it's done.

Chicken Paprika (from Stefi's Grandmother)

Whole chicken, cut up
2 celery stalks, cut up
2 Tbsp. olive oil
1 small onion chopped
1/2 c. flour
1 16-oz. can tomato sauce
2 Tbsp. paprika
1 c. water
8 oz. low-fat sour cream
1 Tbsp. corn starch
salt, pepper to taste

Wash and pat dry chicken. Place flour, salt, pepper in plastic bag, shake chicken in bag to coat. Brown chicken in oil over medium heat. Add celery, onions, tomato sauce, water to cover. Bring to boil, reduce heat, cover and simmer until chicken is tender, approximately 45 minutes. Remove chicken from bone and set aside.

Mix together milk and corn starch. Add to simmering sauce and allow to thicken. Stir in sour cream. Stir in chicken. Serve over dumplings, egg noodles, or rice.

White Chili

1-2 lbs. ground turkey
2-3 cloves garlic
1 lb. bag of dried white navy beans
chili powder
2 small or 1 large onion
salt, white pepper

The night before, soak beans according to package instructions, changing water several times if possible.

In large pot or skillet brown the ground turkey until cooked, add chopped onion and garlic and cook 5 minutes more. Drain and add beans, chili powder, salt, pepper, and any other spices to taste. Cook on low heat one hour, stirring several times.

Enchilada Pie (Ground Turkey)

1 c. chopped red or green pepper
1-2 c. whole kernel corn
2 minced cloves garlic (or 1 small onion)
1 c. pitted black olives, chopped
1 Tbsp. olive oil
8 corn tortillas
1 lb. ground turkey
shredded cheddar or mozzarella cheese
4 tsp. ground cumin
1 jar (10-12 oz.) tomatoes with garlic/onion
1 small can green chilies, rinsed

Accompaniments: shredded lettuce, sprouts, guacamole, sour cream, chopped scallions, diced tomatoes, additional olives, salsa verde

Heat oil in large skillet over medium heat. Sauté bell pepper and garlic or onion for several minutes. Add turkey and crumble to cook thoroughly. Add tomatoes, cumin, and chilies. Simmer 10 minutes to develop flavors. Remove from heat, stir in corn and olives.

To assemble: line the bottom of a 3 qt. glass baking dish with tortillas. Top with half the filling and 1/3 the cheese. Top with tortillas to cover, then rest of the meat filling and 1/3 cheese. Finish with tortillas. Cover with lid or foil. Bake 30 minutes at 350°. Sprinkle on the last 1/3 of the cheese, bake uncovered for 10 minutes more. Remove and let stand for 10 minutes before cutting into wedges. Serve with accompaniments.

Roasted Herbed Vegetables

red-skinned potatoes
celery, carrots
onions (red, yellow, or white)
broccoli
leeks
eggplant
squash (summer, zucchini, acorn, etc.)
herbs/spices to taste, olive oil

Allow about 1–2 cups combined vegetables per person, more if you want leftovers (good for stews and soups, or cold with meat salads). Clean and cube (2" pieces) vegetables, leaving skins on whenever possible. Rub with olive oil, dust with herbs (rosemary, thyme, basil, oregano, parsley, etc.) and/or spices (cayenne, white pepper, etc.) to taste, toss all to coat thoroughly. Cook in hot oven (375-425°) for 20 minutes, stir to brown evenly. Cook 10-20 more minutes until they reach desired doneness (less is better).

Baked Stuffed Zucchini

Zucchini squash (1 large for 2 people)
Marinara or salsa
1 c. chopped steamed vegetables
1/2 c. ricotta and shredded mozzarella cheese
squash (broccoli, peppers, carrots, etc.)

Cut large zucchini in half lengthwise, hollow to within 1/2" of peel. Steam and stuff with chopped steamed vegetables of your choice. Top with 1/4 c. ricotta, 1/2 c. marinara or salsa, and 1/4 c. shredded mozzarella cheese. Bake at 350° for 30-45 minutes until bubbling and golden brown.

Ben's Risotto di Mare

Mince, then sauté in extra virgin olive oil:

2 c. Italian parsley
1 c. celery leaves
8-12 cloves of garlic
1 carrot

Cook for 10 minutes until garlic is soft, then add:

1 1/2 lbs. peeled, de-veined raw shrimp
2 bottles clam juice
2 large cans tomato puree

Let cook 10-20 minutes, remove 1 c. of sauce (for the table), then add:

12 clams in shells (scrub first) and 2 cups uncooked rice

Let cook 30 minutes, stirring occasionally. Serve with green salad and fresh bread. Use reserved sauce as a topping at the table.

Kiss Cookies

3 egg whites
equivalent of 3/4 c. of sugar (DO NOT use honey)
1 1/2 c. coarsely chopped nuts and/or dark chocolate chips

Beat egg whites until stiff, add sweetener slowly, continuing to beat until shiny. Fold in nuts/chips. Drop by spoonfuls onto foiled baking sheet. Bake at 300° for 30 minutes. Let cool on wire rack. Store in airtight container or freeze.

Chocolate Mousse

12 oz. dark chocolate
3 Tbsp. Splenda
2 12-oz. containers Silken tofu
1/4 tsp. vanilla extract
dash cinnamon

In microwave or in top of double boiler, melt chocolate. Stir in Splenda and cinnamon. In blender/food processor, puree tofu with vanilla. Add melted chocolate mixture and puree, scraping down sides of bowl. Pour mixture into small dessert cups, chill several hours before serving. Can be layered with chopped fresh fruit, if desired.

Lassi

1/2 c. yogurt
1/2 c. buttermilk
1/2 c. fruit or fruit juice of your preference

Blend with several ice cubes for a thick delicious, refreshing and nourishing drink. Serves 1.

Brunswick Stew

2-3 lbs. chicken (whole or pieces)
1 bay leaf
1-2 chopped onions
1 tsp. each: marjoram, rosemary,
2-4 cloves garlic, minced
oregano, salt, pepper (to taste)
1 large. jar organic crushed tomatoes or marinara sauce
1 large. bag frozen limas (baby preferred)
6-8 medium red potatoes, diced

Put raw chicken in a large pot, fill with water to barely cover chicken, add about 1 tsp. salt. Bring to boil and simmer for about 90 minutes. Remove chicken from water, put in bowl to cool, then remove meat, discard bones.

Put onions, garlic, tomatoes, potatoes, and spices into chicken stock, heat to slight boil, reduce to simmer. Cook about 1 hour. Add corn and limas, cook half hour more.

Lissa's Fast and Easy Mexican Chicken Stroganoff

3 boneless, skinless chicken breasts
1 small jar salsa
1 pint sliced mushrooms
1 pint low-fat sour cream

Cut chicken into strips. At a low heat, sauté chicken to cook through without browning. When chicken is done, add mushrooms, allow to heat but not brown. (They should be firm and "white.") Add salsa and allow to heat. Add sour cream and stir, allow to heat, but not boil. Serve over rice or pasta, or alone with a green salad.

Chesapeake Bay Crab Cakes

1 lb. fresh crabmeat
1 egg
8 crushed crackers
I Tbsp. Dijon mustard
1/4–1/2 tsp. cayenne
I Tbsp. mayonnaise
chopped fresh parsley
salt to taste

Mix all ingredients, shape into four to six patties. Sauté in olive oil until golden on both sides.

Stir Fry (any meat)

2-3 c. chicken, beef, or pork, slivered
2-3 c. chopped bok choy and/or broccoli
1/4 c. Bragg's liquid aminos
1 c. chopped celery
3 cloves garlic, chopped
1 c. carrots, sliced in thin rounds
1/2 tsp. ground ginger
1 c. squash sliced in thin rounds (opt)
cayenne to taste
1 can sliced water chestnuts, rinsed (optional)
1/4 c. olive oil
1 c. chopped scallions or red onion
sprouts as garnish
1 bell pepper chopped

In deep bowl, mix Bragg's, garlic, and ginger; marinate meat several hours, tossing occasionally. Chop vegetables into a large bowl.

About a half hour before serving time, heat wok to highest setting. When it's as hot as possible, add about half the oil and meat with marinade (stand back!). Stir and turn meat to ensure cooking, but do not over handle. When meat is cooked (about 5-8 minutes, depending on size of pieces and heat of wok), remove it to a clean plate or bowl (not back into marinade dish).

Add more oil to hot wok, and then dump in the bowlful of vegetables. Toss to coat, and then stir occasionally to prevent burning and ensure cooking, but do not over handle or overcook. Vegetables should turn a bright color and still be crisp. Add cooked meat, toss, season to taste. Serve quickly to prevent sogginess, garnish with sprouts, wasabi, Chinese mustard and/or sauces as desired. Put Bragg's on table, too.

Recipes Using Buffalo Meat

Dave's Buffalo Chili
(One of our favorites!)

2 lbs. ground buffalo
1 30.5 oz. can chili beans
1 28 oz. can diced tomatoes
1 pkg. Williams' Chili Seasoning*
1 Tbsp. B-V concentrate
1 large onion
1 can V-8 juice

Brown bison in skillet. Place in crock pot with other ingredients. Slow cook for 6-8 hours.

No salt, msg, or preservatives added.

Buffalo Soup

Knuckle bones (shanks), neck bones, and other bones
2 medium sized onions, sliced
2 carrots, cut in thin strips
3 stalks celery, chopped
2 bay leaves
1 green pepper, sliced
2 Tbsp. lemon juice (divided)
1/2 lb. noodles
1 Tbsp. chopped parsley
salt and pepper

Cover bones with cold water. Bring to a boil and simmer for 1 hour or longer. Skim off fat and scum. Add vegetables, bay leaves and half the lemon juice. Simmer another hour or until meat is tender. Remove bay leaves and bones (there should be about 3 qt. of liquid). Add noodles and boil 15 minutes. Remove from heat and add parsley and rest of the lemon juice. Meat from the bones may be returned to the soup for a more nutritious soup.

Buffalo Casserole with Corn Muffin Top

1 1/2 lbs. ground buffalo
1/8 tsp. pepper
1 Tbsp. chopped onion
1 tsp, salt
1 tsp. chopped parsley
10 1/2 oz. can condensed consommé
1 package corn muffin mix
2 Tbsp. A-1 or Worcestershire sauce
2 Tbsp. butter or margarine

Sauté meat and onion in hot butter in a heavy skillet. Stir in the consommé, parsley, pepper and A-1 or Worcestershire sauce. Spread mixture in a casserole large enough to leave 1-inch space at top. Prepare corn muffin mix and spoon it carefully on top of the casserole, smoothing with a knife. Bake at 325° for 30 minutes.

Mushroom Buffalo Steak

2 lbs. buffalo steak, cut 1" thick
1 small chopped onion
salt and pepper
1 can creamed mushroom soup
2 Tbsp. cooking oil
4 oz. can chopped mushrooms
water

Flour steak, add salt and pepper to both sides. Heat oil in Dutch oven or casserole. Brown onion in hot oil. Remove onion and brown floured steak on both sides. Replace onion and add 1/2 can creamed mushroom soup and 1/2 can of water. Stir in chopped mushrooms. Cover and cook in 325° oven for 2 1/2 hours. Add water if necessary. This may also he cooked on top of the stove at very low heat. Serve over wild rice with pan mushroom sauce.

Buffalo Meatballs

2 c. grated raw potato
4 egg whites
1 1/2 lbs. ground buffalo
1/4 c. butter
2/3 c. chopped onion
3 c. water (divided)

1 clove garlic, minced
2-3 tbsps. cornstarch
2 tsp. salt
2 c. low-fat sour cream
1/2 tsp. pepper
1 tsp. dill seeds
1/4 c. milk

Combine first eight ingredients. Shape into 1-1/2-inch balls and brown slowly in butter. Add 1/2 c. water. Cover and simmer 20 minutes. Remove meatballs. Stir in flour, then remaining water. Simmer to thicken. Reduce heat, stir in sour cream and dill, add meatballs. Heat, do not boil.

Buffalo Coffee Roast
(You won't believe how good this is.)

3-5 lbs. inexpensive cut buffalo meat
garlic or onion
1 c. vinegar
cooking oil
2 c. strong black coffee
2 c. water
salt and pepper

Using a large knife, cut slits completely through the meat. Insert slivers of garlic and/or onion down into the slits.

Pour vinegar over the meat, making sure it runs down into the slits. Put this in refrigerator for 24–48 hours.

When ready to cook, place roast in a big, heavy pot and brown in oil until nearly burned on all sides. Pour coffee over the meat. Add water and cover. Simmer on top of stove for 4-6 hours. Season with salt and pepper 20 minutes before serving.

Buffalo Roast in Plastic Baking Bag

3-4 lbs. buffalo roast
2 Tbsp. flour
1/2 c. red wine vinegar
1/2 c. water
salt
1 bay leaf
8 whole garlic cloves
1 medium onion, diced
1 tsp. thyme

Preheat oven to 325°. Place flour in plastic baking bag and shake until bag is well coated. Place bag in 2-inch deep roasting pan. Pour vinegar into bag and stir until well mixed with flour. Rub roast with salt and put into bag. Add bay leaf, cloves, onion and thyme around meat. Close bag with twist tie. If using a meat thermometer, insert thermometer through bag into center of meat. Make six (6) half-inch slits in top of bag near the twist tie. Cook approximately 2 hours, or until meat is tender. The liquid in the bag is ready to use as gravy or thicken it with flour.

High-Protein, Low-Fat Recipes

Lentil Dinner

1 c.1/2 c. uncooked brown rice
2 cups sliced carrots
3 c. water

1 packet onion soup mix
1 tsp. garlic powder
1 tsp. basil
1 Tbsp. olive oil

Place all ingredients in a large pot. Bring to a boil. Reduce heat, cover, and cook until rice is done, 20 to 30 minutes.

Brown Rice Risotto

1 c. brown rice
1/2 c. chopped onion
1/2 tsp. dried thyme
1/4 tsp. salt
2 c. chicken broth
1/2 c. diced fresh mushrooms

Add brown rice, onion, thyme and salt to 2 cups chicken broth, bring to a boil, reduce heat, cover and simmer 30 minutes. Add diced mushrooms and continue cooking, covered, until all liquid is absorbed and rice is tender, about 45 minutes.

Bulgur Pilaf

1 tsp. oil
1 lb. sliced mushrooms
1/2 c. chopped green onions
1 clove minced garlic
1 c. bulgur
1/2 tsp. salt
2 c. chicken broth

Heat oil and brown mushrooms, green onions and garlic briefly. Stir in bulgur, salt and chicken broth. Bring to a boil, cover and simmer for 20 minutes or until bulgur is tender.

Fried Rice

1 egg plus 1 egg white, beaten together
1 clove minced garlic
1/2 c. thinly sliced celery
1/2 c. chopped green pepper
1/2 c. sliced green onion (reserve tops)
1/2 c. thinly sliced carrot
2 c. cooked rice
1 c. bean sprouts
4 Tbsp. soy sauce
1 Tbsp. lemon juice
1 Tbsp. dry sherry
1/4 tsp. ground ginger

Pour eggs into non-stick frying pan and cook just until set in one large pancake. Remove from pan, cool, cut into thin strips and reserve.

Heat 1 teaspoon oil in pan, then add garlic, celery, green pepper, green onion (not tops) and carrot. Brown, stirring constantly, for about 2 minutes.

Add second teaspoon of oil, then add cooked rice. Stir constantly until heated through and slightly browned. Stir in bean sprouts. Mix together soy sauce, lemon juice, sherry and ginger and pour over all. Place on serving dish and sprinkle with egg strips and tops of green onions.

Legume Soup

1 c. dried white navy beans
1 c. dried small red beans
1 c. dried yellow split peas
1 c. dried green split peas
1 c. dried lentils
1 large chopped onion
2 c. chopped celery
1 clove crushed garlic
1/2 tsp. salt
1 Tbsp. dried basil
1 Tbsp. Worcestershire sauce
2 c. tomato sauce
2 c. stewed tomatoes
4 c. beef broth

Soak dried beans, peas and lentils overnight in water to cover. Add all other ingredients the next day, stir to mix well. Bring to boiling, then lower heat, cover and simmer 3-4 hours or until vegetables are very tender. If soup is too thick, additional broth or water can be added without changing the final flavor.

Mediterranean Macaroni

1/2 lb. lean ground turkey, lamb or beef
1/2 c. chopped onion
1 c. dry macaroni, cooked (4 ounces)
1/2 c. tomato sauce
1/2 tsp. dried thyme
1 tsp. ground cinnamon
1/2 tsp. salt
1/2 c. grated cheddar cheese

Starting with a cold non-stick frying pan, cook ground meat and onion until meat is browned; drain any fat. Stir in cooked macaroni, tomato sauce, thyme, cinnamon and salt.

Spread mixture into an 8" x 8" baking dish. Top with grated cheddar cheese. Bake in a 375° oven about 35 minutes.

Whipped Cottage Cream Cheese

3/4 c. low-fat cottage cheese
3 oz. Neufchatel cream cheese

Rinse the cottage cheese in a strainer and press out any excess moisture. Place in a blender with cream cheese and blend until smooth and creamy. Makes approximately 1 cup.

Belgian Waffles with Strawberries

4 egg whites
1 c. flour
1 1/4 tsp. vanilla extract
2 c. sliced fresh strawberries
2 tsp. undiluted frozen apple juice

Beat egg whites until stiff peaks form. In another bowl, combine the flour, milk and vanilla until smooth, then fold the mixture through the beaten egg whites, taking care not to break down the air bubbles. Spoon the batter into a hot non-stick waffle iron and bake. If waffles stick to Teflon iron, use a light coating of vegetable spray for the first waffle only.

Combine half cup of the sliced strawberries and the apple juice in an electric blender and process the two into a smooth sauce. Pour it over the remaining sliced strawberries and serve as a topping with waffles.

Muesli

1/3 c. old fashioned rolled oats
3 Tbsp. plain, unsweetened yogurt
1/2 c. bananas and peaches, diced
6-8 almonds chopped

Mix in order given. Do not cook. This recipe can be varied by using any whole grain (such as cracked wheat soaked in water for at least 20 minutes), any fruit (fresh, frozen, canned, or dried), and any nuts.

Black Bean Soup

1 Tbsp. olive oil
1 c. chopped onion
1 clove garlic, minced
1 medium green bell pepper, chopped
2 15-oz. cans black beans, rinsed and drained
14-1/2-oz. can stewed tomatoes
10-1/2-oz. can low-sodium chicken broth
1/2 c. picante sauce
1/4 c. water
1 tsp. ground cumin
2 Tbsp. fresh lime juice

Heat oil in a large nonstick saucepan over medium heat until hot. Add onion, garlic, and green pepper; sauté until tender. Add remaining ingredients; stir well. Bring to a boil; reduce heat and simmer, uncovered, 15 minutes. Remove from heat; stir in lime juice.

Tropical Black Beans and Rice

2 tsp. olive oil
1/2 c. finely chopped red onion
1/2 c. orange juice
1/4 c. lemon juice
2 Tbsp. chopped fresh cilantro
1/2 tsp. cayenne pepper
1/2 c. finely chopped red bell pepper
1/2 c. finely chopped green bell pepper
1 medium papaya, peeled, seeded, and diced
2 cloves garlic, minced
2 15-oz. cans black beans, rinsed and drained
5 c. hot cooked rice

Heat oil in a large skillet over medium heat. Add all ingredients except beans and rice. Cook for 5 minutes, stirring occasionally until bell peppers are crisp-tender. Stir in beans. Cook about 5 minutes or until heated through. Serve over rice.

Paul's Lettuce Wrap Chicken Fajitas

12 large Boston lettuce leaves
4 boneless, skinless chicken breast halves
4 pressed garlic cloves
3 Tbs. of vegetable oil
2 Tbs. fresh lime juice
2 bell peppers, sliced (1 red, 1 yellow with ribs and seeds removed)
1 tsp. coarse
1 tsp. cumin salt
1 tsp. ground pepper
1 medium onion, sliced.
1 c. monterey jack cheese
1 c. salsa

In a medium sized bowl combine the lime juice, garlic cumin salt, 2 teaspoons of table salt, and 1/2 teaspoon of ground pepper. Add chicken and be sure to turn the chicken over so that every side is coated.

Heat 2 tablespoons oil in a large skillet over a medium heat. Add the chicken breasts; cook 6-8 minutes per side. Transfer the chicken to a plate and wipe out the pan.

Heat remaining tablespoon of oil in the skillet. Add peppers and onion. Season with salt and pepper. Be sure to toss the peppers frequently until they are crisp-tender, 5-8 minutes usually or just cook until desired.

On a medium sized serving plate align thinly sliced chicken and peppers. Have available the sour cream, salsa, lettuce, cheese for guests to create their perfect fajita. Lime wedges and cilantro make a nice addition.

Dave's Fish Soup

1lb. haddock or cod
5 potatoes
1 sliced onion
2 c. skim evaporated milk
2 c. water
3 Tbsp. fat or margarine
salt and pepper

Wash fish; cut into small pieces, boil 5 minutes. Add sliced onion and potatoes. Cook until fish is done, about 20 minutes. Add milk, water, and fat. Season with salt and pepper. Heat.

Resources

David and Merlene Miller
Miller Associates
800-287-0906
www.Miller-Associates.org

Bridging the Gaps
866-711-1234
www.bridgingthegaps.com

Holder Research Institute
800-490-7714 or 305-535-8803
www.torquerelease.com

Julia Ross
Recovery Systems
www.dietcure.com

Community Addiction Recovery Association
Sacramento, California
916-972-1684

Excel Treatment
Denver, Colorado
303-520-8004
www.exceltreatment.com

American College of Addictionology and Compulsive Disorders
800-490-7714 or 305-535-8803
www.acacd.com

Carol Cummings
Counseling and Mediation Services
Wichita, Kansas
316-269-2322

Power Recovery
Dr. Charles Gant
Karyn Hurley
www.powerrecovery.com

Connected Pathways
Website for women in recovery created by Charles Gant and Karyn
Hurley. Information on the use of nutrients rather than drugs for
recovery.
www.nutrenergy.com

Body of Health
St. Louis, Missouri
Heleine Tobler, nutritional consultant, and Randall Tobler, M.D.
Individual consultation and products for wellness, recovery, and
weight management.
314-749-1545

American Massage Therapy Association
www.amtamassage.org

Biofeedback Certification Institute of America
www.bcia.org

Healing Touch International
www.healingtouch.net

Center for Complementary and Alternative Medicine
www.camra.ucdavis.edu

National Center for Complementary and Alternative Medicine
www.nccam.nih.gov

Joel Lubar
www.brainwavebiofeedback.org

The Upledger Institute
800-233-5880

The International Center for Reiki Training
800-332-8112

The International Institute of Reflexology
813-343-4811

The Rolf Institute of Structural Integration
800-530-8875

Myofascial Release Treatment Centers
1-800-FASCIAL

Rosen Institute
510-845-6606

Endnotes

Chapter 2

1. For information on the reward system of the brain, see:
Kenneth Blum and James Payne, *Alcohol and the Addictive Brain.* (New York: The Free Press, 1991).
Kenneth Blum and Jay M. Holder, *The Reward Deficiency Syndrome.* (Amereon, Ltd., 1998).
G.F. Koob, "Drugs of Abuse: Anatomy, Pharmacology, and Function of Reward Pathways," *Trends in Pharmacological Science* 13 (1992): 177-184.
2. For more information on reward deficiency, see:
Blum, Kenneth et al., "Reward deficiency syndrome (RDS): A biogenic model for the diagnosis and treatment of impulsive, addictive, and compulsive behaviors," *Journal of Psychoactive Drugs* 32 (2000).
David Comings, et al., "Studies of the Potential Role of the Dopamine D1 Receptor Gene in Addictive Behaviors," *Molecular Psychiatry* 2, no. 1 (1997): 44-56.
P.M. Conley and R.S. Sparks, "Molecular Genetics of Alcoholism and Other Addictive/Compulsive Disorders," *Alcohol* 16, no. 1 (1998): 85-91.
3. David Miller and Kenneth Blum, *Overload: Attention Deficit Disorder and the Addictive Brain.* (Kansas City, MO: Andrews and McMeel, 1996).
Ralph Tarter and Kathleen Edwards, "Psychological Factors Associated with the Risk of Alcoholism," *Alcoholism: Clinical and Experimental Research* 12, no. 5 (1988).
4. M.A. Korsten, et al., "High Blood Acetaldehyde Levels After Ethanol Administration: Differences Between Alcoholic and Non-Alcoholic Subjects," *New England Journal of Medicine* 292 (1975): 386-389.
M.A. Schuckit and V. Rayses, "Ethanol Ingestion: Differences in Blood Acetaldehyde Concentrations in Relatives of Alcoholics and Controls," *Science* 203 (1979): 54-55.
5. V.E. Davis and M.J. Walsh, "Alcohol, Amines, and Alkaloids: A

Possible Biochemical Basis for Alcohol Addiction," *Science* 167, no. 920 (1970): 1005-1007.

Chapter 3

1. White House Office of National Drug Control Policy, 1996.
2. For more information on these symptoms, see:

Terence Gorski and Merlene Miller, *Staying Sober: A Guide for Relapse Prevention*. (Independence, MO: Herald House Independence Press, 1986).

3. For more information about Alcoholics Anonymous, see:

Alcoholics Anonymous. (Alcoholics Anonymous World Services, Inc., 1955)

Narcotics Anonymous. (C.A.R.E.N.A. Publishing Co., 1982).

4. For more information about the Disease Model of Alcoholism, see:

I. Maltzman, "Why Alcoholism is a Disease," *Journal of Psychoactive Drugs* 26 (1994): 13-31.

James Milam, "The Alcoholism Revolution," *Professional Counselor* 8 (1992).

Kenneth Blum and James Payne, *Alcohol and the Addictive Brain*. (New York: The Free Press, 1991).

5. Alcoholics Anonymous. (Alcoholics Anonymous World Services, Inc., 1955).
6. Katherine Ketcham and William Asbury, *Beyond the Influence*. (New York: Bantam Books, 2000).

Chapter 4

1. Raymond J. Brown, Kenneth Blum, and Michael Trachtenberg, "Neurodynamics of Relapse Prevention: A Neuronutrient Approach to Outpatient DUI Offenders," *Journal of Psychoactive Drugs* 22, no. 2 (April/June 1990).

G. Kaats, et al., "Effects of Chromium Picolinate Supplementation on Body Composition," *Current Therapeutic Research* 57, no. 10 (1996).

Kenneth Blum and Michael Trachtenberg, "Neurogenic Deficits Caused by Alcoholism: Restoration by SAAVE," *Journal of Psychoactive Drugs* 20 (1988): 297-312.

Kenneth Blum, et al., "Neuronutrient Effects on Weight Loss in Carbohydrate Bingers: An Open Clinical Trial," *Current Therapeutic Research* 48 (1990): 217-233.

Kenneth Blum, et al., "Enkephalinase Inhibition and Precursor Amino Acid Loading Improves Inpatient Treatment of Alcohol and Polydrug Abusers: Double-Blind Placebo-Controlled Study of the Nutritional Adjunct SAAVE," *Alcohol* 5 (1989): 481-493.

Blum, Kenneth et al., "Reward deficiency syndrome (RDS): A biogenic model for the diagnosis and treatment of impulsive, addictive, and compulsive behaviors," *Journal of Psychoactive Drugs* 32 (2000).

Julia Ross, *The Mood Cure*. (New York: Penguin Group, 2002).

Joan Mathews-Larson, *7 Weeks to Sobriety*. (New York: Fawcett Columbine, rev. ed., 1997).

Charles Gant, *End Your Addiction NOW*. (New York: Warner Books, 2002).

2. Billie Jay Sahley and Katherine M. Birkner, *Heal with Amino Acids and Nutrients*. (San Antonio, TX: Pain & Stress Publications, 2001).

3. Seymour Ehrenpreis, *Degradation of Endogenous Opioids: Its Relevance in Human Pathology and Therapy*. (New York: Raven, 1983).

Arnold Fox, *DLPA to End Chronic Pain and Depression*. (New York: Pocketbooks, 1985).

Seymour Ehrenpreis, "Pharmacology of Enkephalinase Inhibitors: Animal and Human Studies," *Acupunct Electrother Res* 10, no. 3 (1985): 203-208.

A.E. Anderson, "Lowering Brain Phenylalanine Levels by Giving Other Large Neutral Amino Acids," *Arch. Neurol* 33, no. 10 (1976): 684-686.

K. Budd, "Use of D-phenylalanine, an Enkephalinase Inhibitor, in the Treatment of Intractable Pain," in: *Advances in Pain Research and Therapy*. J.J. Bonica; J.C. Liebeskind; and D.G. Albe-Fessard, editors. (New York: Raven Press, 1983); 5: 305-308.

G. Donzelle, et al., "Curing Trial of Complicated Oncologic Pain by D-Phenylalanine," *Anesth Analg* 38 (1981): 655-658.

Berman A. Fugh and J.M. Cott, Department of Health Care Sciences, George Washington University School of Medicine and Health Sciences, Washington, DC. "Dietary Supplements and Natural Products as Psychotherapeutic Agents," *Psychosom Med* 61, no. 5 (September 1999): 712-728.

S. Meyers, Lawrence Berkeley National Laboratory, "Use of Neurotransmitter Precursors for Treatment of Depression," *Altern Med Rev* 5, no. 1 (February 2000): 64-71.

"PE and Tyrosine in Double Blinded Studies with People Strung Out on Cocaine," *Journal of Psychoactive Drugs* 20, No. 3 (July-September, 1988): 283-295, 315-331, and 333-336.

Yaryura-Tobias, et al., "Phenylalanine for Endogenous Depression," *J Ortho Psych* 3, No. 2 (1974): 80-81.

4. Eric Braverman, et al., *The Healing Nutrients Within,* (Keats Publishing, Inc., 1997). [Highly recommend. This is the single best referenced source of amino acid information available.]

S. Meyers, "Use of Neurotransmitter Precursors for Treatment of Depression," *Altern Med Rev* 5, No. 1 (February 2000): 64-71.

C. Benkelfat, et al., "Mood-Lowering Effect of Tryptophan Depletion," *Arch Gen Psychiatry* 51 (1994): 687-697.

W.F. Byerley, et al., "5-Hydroxytryptophan: A Review of Its Anti-Depressant Efficacy and Adverse Effects," *J Clin Psychopharmacology* 7, No. 3 (1987).

Farkas, et al., "L-Tryptophan in Depression," *Biol Psych* 11, No. 3 (1976).

E. Hartman and C.L. Spinweber, "Sleep Induced by L-Tryptophan: Effect of Dosages within the Normal Dietary Intake," *J Nervous & Mental Disease* 167, No. 8 (1979).

S.M. Peuschel, et al., "5-Hydroxytryptophan and Pyridoxine," *Am J Dis Child* 134 (1980).

J.E. Reeves and H.W. Laymeyer, "Tryptophan for Insomnia," *JAMA* 262, No. 19 (November 17, 1989).

S.L. Satel, et al., "Tryptophan Depletion: An Attenuation of Cue-Induced Cravings for Cocaine," *Am J Psychiatry* 152, No. 5 (May 1995).

5. L.E. Banderet; H.R. Lieberman; U.S. Army Research Institute of

Environmental Medicine, "Treatment with Tyrosine, a Neurotransmitter Precursor, Reduces Environmental Stress in Humans," *Brain Res Bull* 22, No. 4 (April 1989): 759-762.

J.B. Deijen; J.F. Orlebeke; Department of Psychophysiology, Vrije Universiteit, Amsterdam, The Netherlands, "Effect of Tyrosine on Cognitive Function and Blood Pressure Under Stress," *Brain Res Bull* 33, No. 3 (1994): 319-323.

A.J. Gelenberg and R.J. Wurtman, "L-Tyrosine in Depression," *The Lancet* (October 1980).

I.K. Goldberg, "L-Tyrosine in Depression," *The Lancet* (August 1980).

H. Lehnert, et al., "Neurochemical and Behavioral Consequences of Acute, Uncontrollable Stress: Effects of Dietary Tyrosine," *Brain Res* 303, No. 2 (June 1984): 215-223.

D.K. Reinstein, et al., "Neurochemical and Behavioral Consequences of Stress: Effect of Dietary Tyrosine," *J Amer Col Nutr* 3, No. 3 (1984).

6. Eric Braverman, et al., *The Healing Nutrients Within.* (Keats Publishing, Inc. 1997).

L.L. Rogers, "Glutamine in the Treatment of Alcoholism," *Quarterly Journal of Studies on Alcohol* 18, No. 4 (1957): 581-587.

L.L. Rogers and R.B. Pelton, "Effect of Glutamine on IQ Scores of Mentally Deficient Children," *Texas Reports on Biology and Medicine* 15, No. 1 (1957): 84-90.

Judy Schabert and Nancy Ehrlich, *The Ultimate Nutrient, Glutamine.* (Garden City Park, NY: Avery Publishing, 1994).

R.R.W.J. Van Der Hulst, et al., "Glutamine and Intestinal Immune Cells in Humans," *Journal of Parenteral and Enteral Nutrition* 21, No. 6 (1997): 310-315.

J. Li, et al., "Glutamine Prevents Parenteral Nutrition-Induced Increases in Intestinal Permeability," *Journal of Parenteral and Enteral Nutrition* 18 (1994): 3030-3070.

J.C. Alverdy, "Effects of Glutamine-Supplemented Diets on Immunology of the Gut," *JPEN* 14 (1980): 1095-1135.

M.I. Amores Sánchez and M.A. Medina, "Glutamine, as a Precursor of Glutathione, and Oxidative Stress," *Mol Genet*

Metab 67, No. 2 (June 1999): 100-105.

B.M. Lomaestro and M. Malone, "Glutathione in Health and Disease: Pharmacotherapeutic Issues," *The Annals of Pharmacotherapy* 29 (1995): 1263-1273.

R.F. Grimble, "Effect of Antioxidative Vitamins on Immune Function with Clinical Applications, Institute of Human Nutrition, University of Southampton, U.K.," *Int J Vitam Nutr Res* 67, No. 5 (1997): 312-320.

P. Furst, et al., "Glutamine Dipeptides in Clinical Nutrition, *Nutrition* 13, No. 7/8 (1997): 731-737.

H.G. Windmueller and A.E. Spaeth, "Identification of Ketone Bodies and Glutamine as the Major Respiratory Fuels in vivo for Post-Absorptive Rat Small Intestine," *J Biol Chem* 253 (1978): 69-76.

Ziegler, et al., "Clinical and Metabolic Efficacy of Glutamine-Supplemented Parenteral Nutrition after Bone Marrow Transplantation," *Ann Intern Med* 116 (1992): 821-828.

Hammarqvist, et al., "Addition of Glutamine to Total Parenteral Nutrition after Elective Abdominal Surgery Spares Free Glutamine in Muscle, Counteracts the Fall in Muscle Protein Synthesis and Improves Nitrogen Balance," *Ann Surgery* 209 (1989): 455-461.

N.C. Jackson, et al., Department of Diabetes, Endocrinology and Metabolic Medicine, St. Thomas' Hospital, London, "The Metabolic Consequences of Critical Illness: Acute Effects in Glutamine and Protein Metabolism," *Am J Physiol* 276, No. 1 (January 1999): 163-170.

7. Billie J. Sahley, *GABA: The Anxiety Amino Acid.* (San Antonio, TX: Pain & Stress Publications, 1998).

N.G. Bowery, et al., *GABA: Receptors in Mammalian Function.* (New York: John Wiley & Sons, 1990).

8. Andre Barbeau and Ryan Huxtable, *Taurine.* (New York: Raven Press, 1975).

Timothy Birdsall, "Therapeutic Applications of Taurine," *Alternative Medicine Review* 3, No. 2 (1998): 128-136.

R.J. Huxtable and H. Pasantes-Morales, *Taurine in Nutrition and Neurology.* (New York: Plenium Press, 1981).

R.J. Huxtable, "Physiological Actions of Taurine," *Physiology Review* 72: 101-103.

Herminia Pasantes-Morales, et al., *Taurine: Functional Neurochemistry, Physiology, and Cardiology.* (New York: Wiley-Liss, 1990).

Andre Barbeau and Ryan Huxtable. *Taurine and Neurological Disorders.* (New York: Raven Press, 1978).

9. Julia Ross, *The Diet Cure.* (New York: Penguin Group, 1999).

10. Julia Ross, *The Mood Cure.* (New York: Penguin Group, 2002).

11. Roger J. Williams, *Alcoholism: The Nutritional Approach.* (Austin, TX: University of Texas Press, 1959).

12. Billie Jay Sahley and Katherine M. Birkner, *Heal with Amino Acids and Nutrients.* (San Antonio, TX: Pain & Stress Publications, 2001).

13. Billie Jay Sahley and Katherine M. Birkner, *Heal with Amino Acids and Nutrients.* (San Antonio, TX: Pain & Stress Publications, 2001).

Chapter 6

1. For more information on Acupuncture, see:

Manfred Porkert and Christian Ullman, *Chinese Medicine, Its History, Philosophy, and Practice,* translated and adapted by Mark Howson. (New York: William Morrow and Co., 1988).

2. Isadore Rosenfeld, *Dr. Rosenfeld's Guide to Alternative Medicine.* (New York: Random House, 1996).

3. For more information on Acu-Detox, see:

Alex Brumbaugh, "Acupuncture: New Perspectives in Chemical Dependency Treatment," *The Journal of Substance Abuse Treatment* 10, No. 1 (1993).

Michael Smith, "Acupuncture and Natural Healing in Drug Detoxification," *The American Journal of Acupuncture* 2, No. 7 (1979): 97-106.

4. For more information about Auriculotherapy, see:

Jay M. Holder, et al., "Increasing Retention Rates Among the Chemically Dependent in Residential Treatment:

Auriculotherapy and Subluxation-Based Chiropractic Care," *Molecular Psychiatry* 6, No. 1 (2001).

Jay M. Holder, "Beating Addiction from Bondage to Freedom," *Alternative Medicine* (1999).

Lisa Ann Williamson, "The Secret to Success: Auriculotherapy Treatment Helps Some With Addictions," *Staten Island Advance* (March 18, 2002).

Kenneth Blum, et al., "Reward Deficiency Syndrome: A Biogenetic Model for the Diagnosis and Treatment of Impulsive, Addictive, and Compulsive Behaviors," *Journal of Psychoactive Drugs* 32, Supplement (November 2000): 55-57.

5. Hearing Before a Subcommittee of the Committee on Appropriations, United States Senate, 103rd Congress, First Session, U.S. Government Printing Office.

Chapter 7

1. Jay Holder, et al., "Increasing Retention Rates Among the Chemically Dependent in Residential Treatment: Auriculotherapy and Subluxation-Based Chiropractic Care," *Molecular Psychiatry* 6, No. 1 (February 2001).

2. Jay Holder, "Beating Addiction: From Bondage to Freedom," *Alternative Medicine* (May 1999): 37-40.

3. Jay Holder, "Torque Release Technique: A Subluxation-Based System for a New Scientific Model," *Science* (March/April 1995): 62-66.

Chapter 8

1. M.B. Sterman, "EEG Biofeedback: Physiological Behavior Modification," *Neurosci Biobehav Rev* 5, No. 3 (1981): 405-412.

2. Joel Lubar, et al., "Evaluation of the Effectiveness of EEG Neurofeedback Training for ADHD in a Clinical Setting, as Measured by Changes in T.O.V.A. Scores, Behavioral Ratings, and WISC-R Performance," *Biofeedback and Self-Regulation* 21, (1995): 83-99.

3. M.B. Sterman and L. Friar, "Suppression of Seizures in an Epileptic Following Sensorimotor EEG Feedback Training," *Clinical Neurophysiology* 33 (1972): 89-95.

Sterman, et al., "Biofeedback Training of the Sensorimotor EEG Rhythm in Man: Effect on Epilepsy," *Epilepsia* 15 (1974): 395-416.

4. For more information about Beta Training Neurofeedback, see:

V.J. Monastra, et al., "Assessing Attention Deficit/Hyperactivity Disorder via Quantitative Electroencephalography: An Initial Validation Study," *Neuropsychology* 13 (1999): 424-433.

M.A. Tansey, "Righting the Rhythms of Reason: EEG Biofeedback Training as a Therapeutic Modality in a Clinical Office Setting," *Medical Psychotherapy* 3 (1990): 57-68.

5. *Colorado Springs Gazette*, April 29, 2004.

6. For more about the Alpha-Theta Protocol, see:

E.G. Peniston and P.J. Kulkosky, "Alcoholic Personality and Alpha-Theta Brainwave Training," *Medical Psychotherapy* 4 (1991): 1-14.

7. Tony Stephenson, "Link Between Memory and Neurofeedback," *Imperial College London Reporter* 126 (February 5, 2003)

Chapter 10

1. Connie and Alan Higley, *Reference Guide for Essential Oils.* (Olathe, KS: Abundant Health, 1998).

2. Isadore Rosenfeld, *Dr. Rosenfeld's Guide to Alternative Medicine.* (New York: Random House, 1996).

Chapter 11

1. Jack Trimpey, *The Small Book.* (New York: Dell Publishing, 1989).

Chapter 12

1. January 1996

2. Regina Sara Ryan and John W. Travis, *The Wellness Workbook.* (Berkeley, CA: Ten Speed Press, 1981).
3. Diana W. Guthrie, *Alternative and Complementary Diabetes Care.* (New York: John Wiley & Sons, Inc., 2000).

Chapter 24

1. Matthew Fox, *The Coming of the Cosmic Christ.* (San Francisco: Harper & Row, 1988): 32.
2. Larrene Hagaman, "Building the Temple Within," *The Restoration Witness* (September/October 1990): 4-12.

Suggested Reading

Amen, Daniel, *Healing ADD*. (New York: Putnam, 2001).

Beasley, Joseph D. and Susan Knightly, *Food for Recovery*. (New York: Crown Trade Paperbacks, 1994).

Blum, Kenneth and James Payne, *Alcohol and the Addictive Brain*. (New York: The Free Press, 1991).

Blum, Kenneth and Jay M. Holder, *The Reward Deficiency Syndrome*. (Amereon, Ltd., 1998).

Braly, James and Patrick Holford, *The H Factor Solution*. (North Bergen, NJ: Basic Health Publications, Inc., 2003).

Braverman, Eric and Carl C. Pfeiffer, *The Healing Nutrients Within*. (New Canaan, CT: Keats Publishing, Inc., 1987).

Breggin, Peter, *Talking Back to Ritalin*. (Monroe, ME: Common Courage Press, 1998).

Breggin, Peter, *Toxic Psychiatry*. (New York: St. Martin's Press, 1990).

Davis, Joel, *Endorphins, New Wave of Brain Chemistry*. (New York: The Dial Press, 1984).

DesMaisons, Kathleen, *Potatoes, Not Prozac*. (New York: Simon & Schuster, 1999).

Elkins, Rita, *Solving the Depression Puzzle*. (Pleasant Grove, UT: Woodland Publishing, 2001).

Gant, Charles and Greg Lewis, *End Your Addiction Now*. (New York: Warner Books, 2002).

Gant, Charles, *Alternative and Bionutritional Approaches to ADD and ADHD*. (Syracuse, NY: AFCO, 1997).

Gorski, Terence and Merlene Miller, *Staying Sober: A Guide for Relapse Prevention*. (Independence, MO: Herald House, 1986).

Guthrie, Diana, *Alternative and Complimentary Diabetes Care*. (New York: John Wiley & Sons, 2000).

Higley, Connie and Alan, *Reference Guide for Essential Oils.* (Olathe, KS: Abundant Health, 1998).

Ketcham, Katherine and William Asbury, *Beyond the Influence.* (New York: Bantam Books, 2000).

Mathews-Larson, Joan, *Seven Weeks to Sobriety.* (New York: Fawcett Columbine, 1997).

Miller, David and Kenneth Blum, *Overload: Attention Deficit Disorder and the Addictive Brain.* (Kansas City, MO: Andrews and McNeel, 1996).

Miller, Merlene, Terence T. Gorski, and David K. Miller, *Learning to Live Again.* (Independence, MO: Herald House, 1992).

Pert, Candace B., *Molecules of Emotion.* (New York: Scribner Publishing, 1997).

Reuben, Carolyn, *Cleansing the Body, Mind and Spirit.* (New York: Berkley Books, 1998).

Richardson, Wendy, *The Link Between ADD and Addiction.* (Colorado Springs, CO: Piñon Press, 1997).

Rosenfeld, Isadore, *Dr. Rosenfeld's Guide to Alternative Medicine.* (New York: Random House, 1996).

Ross, Julia, *The Diet Cure.* (New York: Viking, 1999).

Ross, Julia, *The Mood Cure.* (New York: Penguin Books, 2002).

Sahley, Billie and Katherine M. Birkner, *Heal With Amino Acids and Nutrients.* (San Antonio, TX: Pain & Stress Publications, 2001).

Weintraub, Skye, *Natural Treatments for ADD and Hyperactivity.* (Pleasant Grove, UT: Woodland Publishing, 1997).

Williams, Roger J., *The Wonderful World Within You.* (Wichita, KS: Biocommunications Press, 1998).

Young, D. Gary, *Aromatherapy: The Essential Beginning.* (Salt Lake City, UT: Essential Press Publishing, 1995).

Index

About the Authors

Merlene and David Miller are a husband and wife team who have worked in the addiction field for twenty-five years as authors, educators, consultants, and treatment professionals. They are relapse prevention specialists with a deep concern for those for whom traditional treatment has not worked. The Millers currently live in Missouri with their Papillion dog, Sammy.